Karl H. Hertz

Politics Is a Way of Helping People

A Christian Perspective for Times of Crisis

AUGSBURG PUBLISHING HOUSE

Minneapolis, Minnesota

MANUFACTURED IN THE UNITED STATES OF AMERICA

CONTENTS

For

BARBARA

Beloved partner in many enterprises

PREFACE

Two streams of experience converge to shape my reflections on the Christian in political affairs; both streams have contributed fairly equally to form the substance of the chapters that follow.

I have spent most of my adult life in the academic community. Until 1967 I taught sociology in two colleges affiliated with two of the major Lutheran church bodies in the United States. For more than two decades I have found myself frequently called upon to serve as a consultant or in other capacities for groups charged with responsibilities for social witness and reform on a variety of subjects. Although the tasks assigned to me were often primarily descriptive in nature, I was also involved in questions of policy recommendation and policy implementation. If at various places I am critical of how religious organizations discharge tasks of this kind, the criticism can properly be construed as directed to some of my own activities as well as to the work of my colleagues.

Since 1967 I have been Professor of Church and Society at Hamma School of Theology. As a consequence I have had to wrestle much more explicitly with questions of social and political ethics, particularly in the light both of my Lutheran heritage and of crucial events in Lutheran history. At the same time I have become increasingly aware that the issues which academicians find exciting may have little importance either for students for the ministry or for practicing clergy. Meaningful theory must be in touch with practice.

For better than two decades another activity has also claimed varying segments of my time. I have been active in partisan politics. I have rung door bells, gathered signatures for petitions, collected money, served on campaign committees, run for and been elected to public office. I served four years as a member of the City Commission of the City of Springfield, Ohio. I am now and have been for some time the elected member of the County Democratic Central Committee from my precinct. I currently serve as chairperson for both the Central and Executive Committees of the Clark County Democratic Party. I have had the experience of testifying before a committee of the Congress of the United States, as well as involvement in patronage, lobbying, and a whole host of other routine political activities. These practical experiences have, I believe, enriched my academic life, and the academic work has helped me understand somewhat better the nature of political activities.

Two related sets of circumstances provided the immediate stimulus for writing this book. In August, 1972 I had the opportunity to spend a week with a group of lay persons at Camp Lutheridge in North Carolina, discussing the role of the Christian in politics. Those discussions provided the basis for this book.

At the same time my attempts to come to terms with my own Lutheran heritage, especially after I became a member of the Commission on Studies of the Lutheran World Federation, forced me into a critical examination of Luther's doctrine of the two kingdoms. In particular I found myself asking why those who claimed to be its most correct exponents in the German church during the early years of the Nazi dictatorship could find in this heritage a basis for giving support to anti-Semitism. Conclusions as antithetical to the Gospel as those which members of the Erlangen theological faculty reached must rest on flawed premises. Consequently I began to investigate the historical formation of Lutheran ethical theories in both Germany and the United States. That investigation is far from complete.

But the questions which the 1930s raised are also far from settled; they are questions both of the nature of our participation in political life and of the circumstances under which it is necessary to say *No* to public authority. The decades of the 1960s made these issues peculiarly salient for all American Christians. But the questions persist into the 1970s, not only because in the United States the problems which were on the agenda of the 1960s remain unsolved but also because on the international scene, whether in the development of theologies of liberation in Latin America, or in the resistance of two black Lutheran churches in Namibia to the tyranny of South African apartheid, we cannot escape basic political questions. Neither the academic ivory tower nor Christian efforts at noninvolvement will make these problems go away.

I also want to acknowledge three kinds of indebtedness. First I owe deep intellectual debts to James Luther Adams and Daniel J. Boorstin, pre-eminent teachers during my graduate studies at the University of Chicago. I must also acknowledge the continuing stimulus of the unique experiment in theological education going on at Hamma School of Theology. Second, I owe many debts to political associates, in particular to former governor Michael DiSalle who brought to his office a magnificent endowment of compassion for the suffering and the neglected; to John J. Gilligan, the current governor of Ohio, remarkably combining great qualities of humane vision and political astuteness; to two former colleagues on the Springfield City Commission, Maurice K. Baach and Clarence J. Waterman, who in quite different ways illustrated deep concern for the common welfare.

Finally, it is impossible to record the impact of better than a quarter of a century of conversations and frequently common involvement in political activities, sometimes complementary and sometimes identical, with Barbara. Her concerns for integrity, the persistent honesty with which she offered criticism as well as support, and her own deep commitments to freedom, equality, and peace have shaped my thinking in more ways than I can enumerate. Paul, whose years in college covered the restless and tumultuous closing years of the 1960s, not only put his body on the line in some of the protest movements but also raised probing questions about the integrity of our institutions. Judith, who made her first political signs during the John Kennedy campaign in 1960 and who has as a volunteer stuffed thousands of envelopes in the ensuing years (as well as answered telephones, worked in campaign headquarters, and so on) has a knack for raising basic ethical questions about the practices of political parties. No person could ask for better support than these three have given me in cooperation and criticism, commitment and concern.

A word of thanks is also due Betty Webb, who typed and retyped portions of these pages both accurately and patiently.

1

THE PROBLEM OF POLITICAL INVOLVEMENT

Why should Christians have anything to do with politics? The simple truth seems to be that we have no choice. Our common humanity includes entanglement in all kinds of relationships with other persons.

There is nevertheless a Christian witness against taking part in politics as well as one for it. To answer the question simply on the basis of worldly involvement misses both the thrust of the question and the practices of many devout persons. Most of those who answer the question negatively will not deny that they live in the same world with the rest of us. Their answer to the question is aimed at certain very specific kinds of behavior which they hold to be improper. They do hold to a kind of logic which we must examine.

We are here not concerned with extreme positions. The Old Order Amish, the Plymouth Brethren, and certain holiness groups have developed a style of life and a witness reflecting a particular perspective on the world. We must respect these traditions, even though we do not agree with them. We are not concerned with the beliefs and practices of these groups, however, but with the Christians who are apparently in the mainstream. Our problem is with "worldly" Christians who nevertheless insist that "the church" should keep out of politics.

"The gathering storm in the churches," as Jeffrey Hadden has called it, hangs over the mainland of the Protestant world; the outer islands apparently enjoy a different climate. Whatever squalls might strike them, the winds that bring them are not political. It is among Lutherans, Presbyterians, Methodists, Episcopalians — the list is by no means complete — that the grievances have been both loud and frequent. Christians prominent in the community and in the world of business, persons who are registered voters, many of whom hold public offices, lead the chorus of those who question what they call the confusion of religion and politics.

The Problem of Obedience

Common to the thinking of most Christians is a willing submission to constituted authority. "The powers that be," wrote St. Paul, "are ordained of God." (We shall wrestle with this passage later.) "Be subject to all human institutions for the Lord's sake," advised the author of 1 Peter. Thus from the beginning obedience to rulers has been a basic Christian teaching. Almost without exception, Christians must submit to those whom God has set over them. This presumably provides a common ground for all.

During the troubled sixties, first in the civil rights movement and then in the protest against the Vietnam War, a good many of the persons involved in political activity on apparently religious grounds were engaged in civil disobedience. Thus their claims confronted almost directly the received teachings which the churches themselves had inculcated and which many of the devout regarded as in fact divine mandates. Most of the protests against political involvement were aimed at those spokesmen of the churches who appeared to be challenging existing social arrangements, calling into question the constituted authorities. Against this kind of political action many lay people invoked what they considered the authentic Christian tradition going back to apostolic days.

Among American Christians the tradition of obedience is very strong. In one version of the Lutheran tradition obedience to government, no matter how unjust, can almost be called the chief content of teaching on political ethics; Christians are not to reason why; God's word is very clear.

But obedience to constituted authority is only one part of the Protestant heritage. It is not the only tradition which critics of "political clergy" are using. The Reformation provided some further teachings to which American Christians appeal, consciously or unconsciously, to the present day. Calling upon Reformation precedents, many Christians (and non-Christians as well) believe that they can conveniently separate human conduct into two categories, one religious and the other non-religious. Thus prayers, attendance at worship, helping the poor through Christian charities, and similar activities are clearly religious; they are the business of the church and of the clergy. But voting, passing laws, regulating the marketplace, taking care of the poor through tax monies, dealing with social inequalities, and so on are clearly not religious activities. This position, neatly dividing the world into two parts, is not a prerogative of the devout; a good many explicitly secular persons also subscribe to this view.

The differences between groups committed to stricter rules of non-participation and the others is partly a matter of where the line is drawn; in other words, of what kinds of activities are out of bounds or, if not themselves questionable, are so fraught with temptation that Christians should avoid them. In addition, the more conservative groups also insist upon a stricter control over their members.

Some Christians draw the line not only in a different place but also in a different way. They believe some forms of conduct so contrary to the will of God that these actions should be forbidden to all citizens. Thus they are willing to identify their partisan votes and their vested interests with the cause of Christianity itself. At the same time they protest quite loudly their loyalty to the separation of church and state. They apparently want the best of both worlds.

A historical example will serve to illustrate this second approach. Before and during the Civil War some Northern Methodist leaders played key roles in the formation of the Republican party. After the war Northern Methodists with military help not only occupied key positions in the military governments of the former rebel states, but they also used military power to take possession of church buildings and devote them to more loyal religious uses.

One important change has occurred since the middle of the last century. Today we are apparently more likely to accept approval of the status quo as religiously proper, its criticism or the advocacy of new positions as questionable. Religious organizations should not involve themselves in programs of social innovation.

The prohibition crusade provides the best example of a long continued Protestant effort to impose a moral mandate on the entire population. For many devout persons this issue even today is far from dead. Once one gets into questions of personal conduct, then one can indeed put together a list of offenses against righteousness for which both individuals and church groups have demanded restrictive legislation. They were not, in their own eyes, mixing religion and politics, surely not offending against separation of church and state. They had simply taken a position in behalf of public decency (on sex offenses, gambling, Sunday sales, obscene movies, the teaching of evolution, pornographic literature). Surely any right-minded Christian must agree.

More striking as a "moral cause" in our day is the abortion controversy. Almost no religious group can avoid taking a stand by appealing to the separation principle; in fact, both sides are quite convinced that theirs is the Christian position and that their opponents are somehow benighted. What is at issue is of greatest importance: our understanding of human life. Whenever the question gets into the political arena, emotions run high, misunderstandings abound, and other considerations become secondary.

By cataloging issues we can quickly illustrate the ambiguities which some of these questions contain, but we will not get at the more important question of the underlying principles. Advocates of both positions believe themselves to be following classic Protestant teachings. A central Reformation achievement was certainly untangling the spiritual and the worldly realms from one another. Especially in the United States, Protestant Christians have seen separation of church and state as a simple development of this primary distinction. Every generation of Americans has fought over this principle. The debates have been long, and they have not yet ended. While in our own day the line is drawn somewhat differently than in the past, the loyalty which the principle claims remains a major fact of American political life.

In isolating the distinction between the two realms, in looking at the question of religion and politics we must recognize the existence of different lines of inheritance and different forms of expressions. Sometimes the accent will fall on obedience; sometimes it will fall on separation. In either instance political ethics requires carefully drawing the line between what belongs to God and what belongs to Caesar. This distinction is not necessarily identical with the difference between public morality and private morality.

What Luther Taught

Much of what American Protestants take for granted rests on a misreading of the Reformation, in particular of Luther. But this information does not tell us how we got off the track. To get at that question, we need to look at some history.

In claiming Luther as an ancestor and a warrant for their positions, Protestants are both right and wrong. They are right in their understanding that Luther articulated a major protest against an improper mixture of matters of worldly concern and matters of faith. They are even right that some of his language, torn out of its sixteenth century context, may seem to justify the passive attitudes of many contemporary believers, especially the more conservative and the more devout. But in overlooking the historical context of Luther's day and the complexities of European political history in the generations that followed, Protestants of the passive political persuasion have oversimplified and frequently distorted Luther's analysis. Furthermore, it is important not to read back into Luther in too direct a way the forms which ethical teachings on political questions took in some of the churches that followed Calvin more closely than Luther.

We must look for two kinds of sources in Luther's writings. We have, first of all, as major sources for his reflections about the role of the Christian and of the church in the world, some of his important polemical tracts. These came out of the heat of controversy, were directed at specific abuses, and must be understood in their historical setting. For example, when in his tract on *Temporal Authority,* Luther advises a form of passive civil disobedience, a willingness to suffer for the faith, we must ask seriously whether in fact other options were open to the Christians of that day. No Civil Liberties Union was available to take their case to the courts. No possibility existed for forming a political organization to fight an unjust ruler. The choices were very limited. Even to assert that the individual believer must serve conscience first could be construed as a politically dangerous doctrine.

A second source of Luther's teachings must be found in his biblical commentaries and in the instructional materials he prepared for Christian people. In both instances Luther's concerns were more pastoral than political, more concerned with the immediate situation than with developing a systematic theology. Later generations did the systematizing, often rather selectively, generally in terms of their own political situations.

Luther clearly wanted to get rid of ecclesiastical interference in political affairs, the whole web of political intrigue and counter-intrigue in which pope, bishops, and other religious dignitaries of his time were involved. He wanted them to get out of this kind of activity, not because political functions were stamped with some kind of sinfulness peculiar to them, but simply because all these involvements kept these persons from fulfilling their proper calling, the proclamation of the gospel, the spiritual oversight over the faithful. Luther also wanted secular rulers to quit mixing in religious matters. They had their proper duties to perform; they had enough work to keep them busy if they indeed would measure up to what God expected of earthly magistrates.

Luther's motives were thus clearly pastoral. They can be echoed today when lay persons complain that ministers should stick to the gospel. This seems clear enough. In making the distinction between the religious and the worldly, we have not, however, defined the content of the obligations in both. Luther could indeed turn the protest back upon the laity; that is, let lay Christians who demand that the pastor not neglect the proper duties owed to the gospel remember that the same rule requires lay persons to be equally faithful *under God* in their responsibilities. His treatise *To the Christian Nobility* contained just such instructions, an undertaking he judged as futile three years later, when he noted that these persons "will continue to be princes and never become Christians."

I have sneaked in a phrase, very familiar as a piece of political liturgy: *under God*. We need to look at this phrase. Understanding what the phrase implies is critical for the development of any political ethic from a Christian perspective. It is equally important to note its centrality in Luther's thought. Luther did not see the worldly employments of Christians as in any sense independent of divine authority. Luther would not recognize a secular realm in the modern sense. All human activity is subject to God's rule; the differences lie in the way in which different activities are "under God."

But if all activities are "under God," then we must also remember that for Luther this clearly means under the God about whom the Scriptures testify, the Father of our Lord Jesus Christ. Then indeed it may very well be true that the Christian pastor and indeed the organized religious group must have something to say about how earthly duties are carried out, both individually and corporately. On this point Luther is quite clear: there are improper ways for the clergy and the churches to speak on political questions, but there are also proper ones.

Luther's practice in political questions is highly significant. Far from being silent on controversial issues, he often had specific instructions to give: on keeping children in school, on the nature of a just war, on how to deal with the rebellious peasants. Always two concerns were paramount: the proper activity of magistrates is to serve justice and provide for human welfare. Within the sphere of civil affairs, whether among Christians or non-Christians, simple common sense and the use of reason clearly served to point out what was needed.

The second concern was both more crucial and more central for Luther: the cause of the gospel cannot be identified with any social, political, or economic movement, *no matter how just.* The criteria for judging the validity of such a movement cannot be found in the gospel as such. This does not mean that the criteria are secular, or that justice is a matter to be determined on non-religious grounds. Nor does it mean that Christians cannot or should not choose. But we must understand that the full sweep of the Word of God includes both believers and unbelievers, that those affairs of human societies which involve all of us as fellow human beings must not be determined by criteria which only some of us can meet; public affairs are not matters of faith; they are clearly matters of justice. Justice is as much a divine concern as faith, but it is a concern expressed in a different way, recognizing the limits within which political affairs are to be handled.

What has been said about Luther's general stance on political questions could almost as easily have been said about Calvin's views. No more than Luther did he subscribe to a doctrine of separation of church and state in the modern sense. Yet in keeping with the Protestant critique of the Roman church, Calvin and his followers also clearly distinguished the roles of the clergy from those of the magistrates. Secular rulers were to deal only with external affairs. The human soul was outside their jurisdiction.

We may find it difficult to comprehend at times that sixteenth century thinkers could really believe that they were dealing with bodies and souls in two different ways because we no longer see reality through the conceptual frameworks they found natural. Yet the dichotomies they insisted on persist in our language and in our behavior. The sixteenth century Christian who could hand a heretic over to the magistrates as a common criminal no more saw himself violating freedom of conscience than the twentieth century white middle class person who wants the police to crack down on black demonstrators believes himself to be a white racist. Our definitions are ways of setting limits on what we see and how we understand what we see. The distinction which the Reformers drew between the jurisdictions of ecclesiastical and political authorities became the apparently inviolable boundary between public and private morality in our day.

How this came about is a question of history, both intellectual and political, the details of which need not concern us here. But there is one facet of the distinction that remains to be noted. To define the problem, as we often do, as one of church and state, not only oversimplifies but gravely distorts what the Reformers (Luther, Calvin, and many others) had to say about the daily lives of believers. In their day one could still in some degree define the world of social reality as essentially divided into two realms, church and empire, pope and emperor, the spiritual and the secular swords. Ideas and institutions corresponded to one another.

Our contemporary situation is much more complex, and it will not do to reduce the world to two parts, no matter how related. The familiar dualisms of the swords or the kingdoms had meaning in societies in which church and state towered above all else as the dominant institutional realities. But even where an "establishment" still exists legally, a pluralistic social order has in fact replaced the old structures. The contemporary social world is a vast complex of many organizations and an almost infinite multitude of minor ones, voluntary or semi-compulsory, varying from local associations to national and international corporate bureaucracies.

If a dichotomy is still valid, that dichotomy cannot order life in terms of church and state — far too much would be omitted. We might distinguish church and community, but once we make this distinction, we are in trouble. Two swords and two kingdoms had meaningful institutional referents; they existed alongside one another in organized form. But within the community we do not have *church* (singular) but *churches* — of diverse traditions, sizes, and theological persuasions. Within the community we have many kinds of organizations. Our relations and our problems are multilateral.

The distinction between the two realms easily although incorrectly became equated with the distinction between law and gospel, the differentiation of love and justice. These theological discriminations had psychological as well as sociological counterparts. Thus it became easy to separate the inner from the outer, the private from the public, the domain of personal kindness from the domain of official rigor. Thus it was easy for most highly committed Christians voluntarily to withdraw from political participation.

Any interpretation which tries to divide the world into two neat halves, with all the good guys on one side and all the bad guys on the other (a temptation to which Luther also succumbed at times) must be rejected. To understand Luther's distinctions we need to look much more closely at the questions Luther addressed himself to and the kind of answers which he gave.

As an initial source for Luther's questions I suggest taking the two fundamental principles Luther asserted in a treatise of 1520, the treatise on *The Freedom of a Christian:*

1) The Christian is a perfectly free Lord of all, subject to none.

2) The Christian is a perfectly dutiful servant of all, subject to all.

"These two theses," as Luther admits, "seem to contradict each other. If, however," he continues, "they should be found to fit together they would serve our purpose beautifully." Taken together the theses reflect a basic characteristic of Lutheran theology, namely, that it is *in its very essence dialectical*. In Lutheran theology we are constantly engaged in trying to bring together apparent opposites and out of their encounter to extract fundamental assertions about the life of faith. In the doctrine of the sacraments, for example, Lutherans neither go all the way with the Roman view that transforms earthly elements into divine substances nor do they stop short with the radical Reformed view that claims that nothing happens except some eating and drinking accompanied by devout reflection on the memory of our Lord. Lutherans affirm the real presence "in, with, and under" the earthly elements. They bring the divine and the earthly together without sacrificing the reality of either.

The dialectic also has a political expression. Fundamentally Luther sees the Christian standing in both realms, the religious and the worldly. (This is why spatial metaphors are fundamentally wrong.) This simultaneous location constitutes both dilemma and opportunity for the Christian. Far from counseling Christian withdrawal from the world, Luther and his fellow reformers called believers back into the world. It was in the world and at worldly tasks that the Christian was to live the life of faith. He could not divide the world into two parts.

How was the Christian to do this? Luther had no set of detailed prescriptions. The freedom of the gospel indeed precludes setting up new legal codes, although Lutherans as well as other Christians have time and time again succumbed to this temptation. Luther did however see in the gospel a simple paradigm from which the Christian could find guidance for his life. The fundamental distinction in the life of faith is between what I do for myself and what I do for others, for my neighbor. For myself I am to suffer injustice quietly, to accept persecution, oppression, cruelty. But on behalf of my neighbor in need, when he is oppressed, when he suffers injustice, if he is hungry, imprisoned, naked, and so on, I am to do everything I can. As Luther says, "Love of neighbor is not concerned about its own; it considers not how great or how humble, but how profitable and needful the works are for neighbor or community."

The arena for this activity in behalf of the neighbor is the world, the world in all its complexity, including the world of politics. The life of faith requires not only the response of worship, which is what I owe to God, but it also calls forth the response of helpfulness in the broadest sense, which is what I owe to my neighbor.

Politics is a way of helping people; this is why Christians may find in political activity a very legitimate vocation. What we have in Luther's teaching is quite simply the Reformation doctrine of good works. But these works are not redemptive; they flow from faith.

What I do in politics, what I do in any area of social life, is never salvatory; my deeds of neighborly helpfulness are not ways of earning a heavenly reward. Good works are the fruit of faith; for believers, they ought to be "doing what comes naturally." A measure of the distortion which Lutheran ethics has undergone — a distortion in which much of Protestant ethics has shared — has been the degree to which this clear pastoral injunction of Luther's has been forgotten, indeed implicitly and explicitly denied in the area of public life. Protestants, Lutherans in particular, have often acted as if good works were optional.

Let me add a second disclaimer and thus come to the heart of the Lutheran dialectic. In serving my neighbor, I may indeed be acting justly but I dare not claim any particular virtuousness or holiness before God. For in Luther's magnificent phrase, we are always simultaneously saints and sinners, at the same time justified and yet sinful. The Lutheran *simul* (taken from the Latin expression, *simul justus et peccator*) is central to the dialectical understanding of the gospel; it provides, as I shall try to suggest, safeguards against particular kinds of ideological nonsense in the political and social arenas.

Lutheran theology also contains an explicit political dialectic, one that has been generally ignored. We have presumably long known about the universal priesthood of believers. Vatican II underlined this doctrine with its strong words about the role of "the People of God." Despite all the brave words, however, in most main line Protestant denominations the universal priesthood has been very effectively neglected. One of the reasons for this neglect has been our failure to bring that priesthood into creative relationship with a second structural principle, the affirmation of the need for a public ministry. These two affirmations belong together; we must simultaneously affirm public ministry and universal priesthood.

Lutheran history is somewhat different from that of many other Protestant groups in its openness to structural variety. Almost every form of church government found anywhere in Protestantism can also be found among Lutherans; we have run the gamut from high episcopalian polities with traditions of apostolic succession to congregationally organized churches with a deep suspicion of an educated clergy. This wide sweep of organizational forms should have called to our attention the strange combination of authority and democracy which is the Reformation heritage. Even in the utterances of Luther we find both: consider the political implications of *The Freedom of a Christian* as a source of democratic impulses over against *Temporal Authority* with its claims for the authority of the magistrates.

We have here the central problem of the twentieth century: how shall authority and democracy co-exist? What is the proper balance between freedom and order? In what respects is hierarchy a proper principle of organization? Where must collegiality be primary?

These are not just questions for the churches; they are the fundamental questions raised in the revolutionary events of our century; they are the questions every oppressed minority has been asking. Yet all of these questions are implicit in the simultaneous affirmation of both public ministry and universal priesthood.

The great political problem in the church and in public life is how to bring freedom and order, hierarchy and collegiality into fruitful and meaningful relationship with one another. "Following Pascal," as James Luther Adams has said, "we might call this the ethos of opposite virtues. According to him, the Christian has the obligation to exhibit opposite virtues and to occupy the distance in between. That is, we confront the obligation to pursue at the same time the opposite virtues of freedom and order, of freedom and equality, of participation and privacy, of justice and mercy." During most of Christian history this strategy has been largely ignored. We have tended to select one or the other principle for almost exclusive emphasis. Because this dialectic gets at the heart of the question of authority, and at the roles of clergy and laity in the believing community, we can see in it a clue for understanding the history of the Christian church. In a sense the battle between emperor and pope was one form of the struggle of the laity against priestly control. The Reformation — including some of the battles fought in Geneva and especially the Anabaptist left wing — gave lay resistance to ecclesiastical autocracy a major impetus. In Protestant history the struggle has continued to our day; the universal priesthood, no matter how suppressed or distorted, keeps asserting itself. For some contemporary Roman Catholics the role of the laity has also become a burning issue.

In introducing these questions we have moved from concern with the conduct of the individual believer to questions of the organized religious group. We are approaching questions of structure. Before we focus on structure itself, however, we need to look at the role assigned to the individual Christian within ecclesiastical and communal structures. How do we live the life of faith within the believing community? in the larger community?

Here the Reformation heritage offers us both guidance and

problems. Because the Reformers inherited a mode of speech about human nature that rested upon the distinction between inner and outer, soul and body, in Greek not in biblical terms, they tended to identify the life of faith with inner events, worldly concerns with outer events. Practice was not always consistent with this distinction; nevertheless, a very misleading generalization grew up distinguishing between my activities as a person and my duties as an office-holder.

Presumably then the gospel injunctions of love, forgiveness, and so on were applicable only in private life, and the public affairs of men became matters to be attended to according to the laws and conventions of justice. In private life collegiality, equality, and freedom were the norm (but the administrative structure of the church as an external element was hierarchical); political life was a matter of obedience and authority. Thus law and gospel, love and justice were torn apart and assigned to different realms; by this intellectual surgery one could avoid meeting the dialectical togetherness of these elements head-on.

Generations of Protestants neatly swallowed the divided world. Yet the practice and the writings of the reformers suggest that the distinctions could not be drawn in this convenient way. Justice for Luther and his fellow reformers was as much God's concern, therefore a Christian responsibility, a part of the life of faith, as forgiveness. The issue was not dividing the word into sacred and secular realms, but when and how justice and forgiveness were appropriate. We must not forget that for Luther love as mutual concern for the other person's rights and natural law, "with which all reason is filled," belonged together as qualities of a just administration. His admonitions to princes and magistrates in secular authority constantly come back to these themes. Yet from his point of view in such matters law was at work, not the gospel.

The easy distinction between what I can do as a person in informal and intimate relationships and what I can do as an office-holder under pressure of law and organizational rules and procedures has persisted in Christian ethics to this day.

The distinction seems to limit a valid Christian ethic to the realm of personal conduct. While Ernst Troeltsch in his *Social Teachings* aimed his critical shafts particularly at Luther, many other Christian teachers must be included among the protagonists of this apparently valid distinction.

The distinction is attractive because it contains a half-truth. In fact every human role, every human relationship to other persons, contains social constraints; informal constraints are sometimes more difficult to resist than formal ones. At the same time the dimension of the personal dare not be removed from any office, no matter how formal. Nor is it necessarily easier to be Christian in one's intimate relationships. The largest percentage of murders committed in our society involve persons bound together in ties of intimacy, often husband and wife. Nor is it always easier to forgive one whom one has loved deeply than to show mercy to a stranger. Our human experience challenges the dichotomy; the personal and the official dare not be separated.

Is not the heart of our contemporary dissatisfaction with big organizations, with bureaucracy, the disappearance of the personal from our public dealings with one another? For me at least one of the most terrifying developments in military technology has been the mechanization of killing, its reduction to an impersonal routine carried on at a distance.

Here political involvement plays a not inconsequential role. What I find myself doing as a party official, especially in matters of patronage, is bringing an element of personhood back into play. Personal loyalty is very important in American politics. Indeed political parties have always acknowledged the importance of personal relationships. Party channels of intervention are one way in which, for good or ill, we humanize bureaucracies. Party leaders at their best are always concerned for the personal welfare of their constituents. The patronage system, for example, constantly invokes personal considerations over against the impersonality of civil service.

We also know the temptation of the personal in politics. Friendship corrupts. Neither in our personal capacities nor as office-holders do we escape the *simul*, the insidious poison that turns justice into injustice, honesty into corruption. I dare not excuse any action in any organizational setting by invoking the familiar liturgy that "politics is politics" or "business is business," that I cannot afford to be Christian in my public actions. The Watergate hearings offer eloquent testimony about what happens to "good" persons when they let "official" demands to be part of "the team" silence personal moral scruples.

Let me take the classic example, cited since Luther's day. This is the instance of the Christian as a judge, called upon to execute judgment rather than to extend forgiveness. But we must carry the analysis further than this general statement. The Christian serving as a judge must sentence a convicted criminal not out of some slavish obedience to "law" but because his concern for the welfare of all ("for others") in an imperfect social order requires the kind of order and authority that law represents. This is not a matter for self-righteous pride, but for a searching of conscience. The judge must ask himself—as modern criminal law often makes possible—"What is the right course of action in this instance both for this person before me and for the welfare of all?" He must deal with the individual criminal as a person, as a human being, not simply as some one falling under a legal category which can furnish a predetermined outcome. Many Christians sitting on the bench have recognized, for example, that putting the chronic alcoholic behind bars helps neither him nor the community. Many judges are active in using the powers and prestige of their office to develop better ways of dealing with this and similar problems. All of them in varying ways make use of provisions for suspending sentences, granting probation, and so on, tempering justice with mercy, hopefully always with an eye to what is best for the neighbor, namely, the person they must sentence. For a judge to lose his sense of personhood is to surrender his humanity.

The principle of the *simul* reminds us that no one can exercise an office without entanglement in the injustices of our society. The *simul* also reminds us that in our private lives we are equally entangled. In marriage, in sexual relationships, in family relationships, we cannot strip ourselves of our social roles; we do not relate to one another as naked souls — indeed in our nakedness we sometimes relate most poorly. "Love" has too often served as a cover for exploitation, injustice of the worst sort, between men and women, parents and children, and among friends. We should not have needed the women's liberation movement to remind us of this basic fact.

Let me rephrase what has apparently been separated in the distinction between person and office. I dare not hide my personhood in my office; nor do I have the right to neglect the duties of my office in behalf of some higher personhood. I must hold these in dialectical tension.

Through my public office, as well as in my other capacities, I must as a Christian always take seriously the injunction to care for my neighbor. This is why Christians belong in politics. Politics is a way of helping people.

2

WITNESS IS INESCAPABLE

The storms besetting the mainline Protestant religious groups are no new phenomenon. The very diversity of the American denominations testifies to a lack of consensus on questions of faith and life. Not all differences concern basic principles, yet when differences run as deep as they have in our day, it may be well to get at some of the fundamental reasons why presumably committed Christians are locked into seemingly irreconcilable positions.

Two characteristics of the discussions seem paramount: a confusion about what constitutes a faithful Christian life before God; and a lack of understanding of what organized Christian commitment implies. The individual Christian hears demands about how he should be conducting his personal life; he is not sure in what sense these demands are obligatory, nor to what degree these requirements belong to his life of faith, what is included within the scope of his commitment, particularly in the affairs of the marketplace and the community, his external relationships to neighbors and fellow human beings.

In translating faith into life, individual church members can rightly claim that the teachers of the church have been sending out confusing signals. The pulpit is by no means the only source of religious instruction. Popular devotional literature, which the churches themselves provide through their publication enterprises but which is also available from other sources, free lance religious publishers, radio preachers, and the like, contributes to the spiritual formation of the religiously inclined. So does Sunday school literature, especially perhaps the materials used in the adult Sunday school classes, as filtered through the religious understanding of the thousands of volunteer teachers; so finally does the hymnody of the church.

None of this instruction takes place in a religious or social vacuum. To what degree understandings of the Christian life formed in earlier generations are passed on in the early instruction of the child in the home, the circle of friends, and in the early Sunday school years — or through released time religious instruction of various kinds, is hard to determine. But the results of social surveys suggest that many of these beliefs are still strongly held. Furthermore, partly through the format of public news reporting "true religion" in the public mind continues to be identified with "that old time religion"; the platitudes of Billy Graham are considered more faithful to the biblical witness than the moral insights of Reinhold Niebuhr.

Most secular observers of changes in religious teachings and practices take a very unhistorical view of what they see. Religious positions which are relatively new in Christian history (e.g., snake-handling cults) are described as examples of New Testament Christianity or "that old time religion." "Fundamentalism," for example, far from being a return to first century Christianity, is actually a late nineteenth century development. Awareness of the historical embeddedness of knowledge, scientific as well as religious, is still very new, even among liberals. From a theological viewpoint the embeddedness of knowledge in its contexts is another illustration of the *simul,* the intertwining of divine and human; such embeddedness is not to be confused with certain philosophical notions of relativism. This historical understanding has in addition generally escaped the popular press, many of whose practitioners (not unlike many ex-conservatives turned anti-conservatives in other circles) confuse what was taught them in Sunday school with "the faith once delivered to the saints."

Devotionalism and Ethics

One consequence of this kind of popular understanding of religion is that in the minds of many lay people one facet of the Christian life tends to be identified with the entire scope of Christian ethics. The individual-centered pattern of piety, which many think of as the authentic Christian ethic, is in fact also a development of the latter half of the nineteenth century, when American Protestants turned away from kingdom-building to holiness. Devotionalism, which deals with the individual's relationship to God, took priority over other understandings of the Christian life. Being devout became confused with being ethical; in fact, devotionalism in many ways swallowed up ethics.

Most ethical and devotional literature fails to distinguish clearly between these two equally necessary dimensions of the life of faith. Quite frequently, in fact, they are treated as exclusive alternatives; so we are presumably forced to choose between the cultivation of certain religious virtues, prayer and meditation, personal holiness before God, on the one hand, and social involvement, compassionate activity and witness in behalf of the neighbor, prophetic demands for social justice, on the other hand. Most of the time in the popular literature of Protestantism (including its hymnody) the instruction of the faithful has taken the form of spiritual formation, not ethical enlightenment. Thus we are urged to praise, to give thanks, to cultivate the inner life, to be patient in suffering, to accept adversity, to lift up our eyes to the hills in contemplation, to consecrate ourselves to the service of God, to be faithful in our pilgrimage — and having done these things, presumably we have defined the Christian life.

The confusion of devotionalism with ethics is not unrelated to the second confusion in the Protestant translation of faith into life, the failure to understand the related categories of personal conduct and official duty, to bring together the private and the public spheres of life. Even in our social pronouncements, in what we consider social ethics, we have been almost exclusively person-centered; we have not come to grips with either the question of organizational capabilities or of organizational limitations.

Thus to develop a proper political ethic we must clarify two related questions: How do we understand the relationship between the devotional life and ethical commitment? How can we distinguish between what the individual Christian can and should do in political life and what organized religious groups can and should do? We need in this connection also to clarify our understanding of the nature of religious commitments and of the roles of religious organizations, as well as the relationships of believers and church to one another. We must spell out these answers in sociological as well as in theological terms. Above all, we need to be honest about what we can ask of the individual Christian.

Quite obviously, the development of patterns of devotionalism in individual church members contributes significantly to the survival of religious organizations. Until recently the development of personal piety, at least in moderate amounts and in the inoffensive forms of church attendance, respectable behavior, and personal kindness probably also helped to improve one's status in the eyes of the neighbor. Beyond this, however, some research data suggest that persons devotionally oriented may also be more inclined to be open to concerns for the exploited and the oppressed. Devotionalism rather than orthodoxy seems to provide the link between faith and action.

The primary concern of this study is with the ethical not the devotional. But this concern does not in any sense downgrade the importance of a Christian's devotional life. Bible reading, prayer, repentance, church attendance, meditation, or the cultivation of our awareness of God's presence count. Indeed faith and the exercise of faith, which is what devotionalism is, must precede good works.

Nor is survival in and of itself a goal to be condemned. Unless religious organizations survive, they will not of course be able to carry out their basic mission. Part of that mission is the proclamation of the good news which calls into being a company of the faithful, that is, the gathering of the people of God into visible assemblies for religious worship, for celebration and mutual edification.

But neither individuals nor organizations are free from behavior which corrupts and distorts what they are doing. This is what Luther's *simul,* his insistence that we are always both sinners and saints, constantly serves to keep before our attention. It is one thing to cultivate personal piety; it is another matter altogether to define piety as the full measure of what the life of faith is. It is surely understandable when religious groups concern themselves with questions of survival; it is questionable whether they deserve to survive when internal concerns dominate both their agendas and their budgets.

There is also work to be done in the world, and Christians have a responsibility to do that work, not just to get ready to do it. The Christian life is lived not only in relationship to God and before God; it is also lived in relationship to the world, our neighbors, and the organized structures of our communities. For as Christians we cannot escape the world. How to live in the world is the burden of Christian ethics. Christian ethics is something beyond, indeed different from though not unrelated to, the cultivation of personal religiosity.

The Christian calling to be "the servant of all" thus calls for something more than the practice of personal virtue. Nowhere did the pietistic and evangelical revivals and the holiness movements move farther away from the Reformation than in their preoccupation with my personal holiness, with my personal development as a Christian.

We can admit that historically good reasons existed for the development of these protests against a cold intellectualism, an apparently dead formalism, in Protestantism. The focus on self-improvement, however, the concern with one's own religious experience, a hallmark of nineteenth century Romanticism and religious awakenings, reflected what Luther would label the classic religious sin, the *incurvatus in se* quality of much Christian religiosity. Luther knew from his own experience what it meant to strive for holiness; he knew self-examination, ascetic discipline, regular spiritual exercises in the monastery. From this experience he could clearly document the danger that comes to the religious consciousness that is turned in upon itself. Because that religious consciousness has made the human being the focus of its attention, it has taken its eyes off the saving work of Christ. It has substituted a new bondage for the liberty which Christ gives. Thus the Christian life is turned in the wrong direction.

One need not spend much time reading the instructional and devotional literature even of many of the mainline denominations to discover that in various ways the weight of directives is upon self-centeredness, upon the self, its vicissitudes and improvement. The bulk of the literature which comes from the non-denominational publishers simply reinforces this thrust. Thus in many places the private devotional literature, the Sunday school materials — perhaps even many of the Sunday sermons — run contrary to the calls for commitment which may come from commissions on social concerns. No wonder the individual Christian is confused; his religious teachers are giving him contradictory signals.

Self-centeredness it should be reiterated is by no means a monopoly of religiously conservative or holiness groups. A good deal of liberalism, from the days of Henry Ward Beecher to the present, has cultivated a piety of personal growth whose differences with the holiness groups were more matters of intensity than of intent. In more recent times liberalism often has seemed to find more resources for moral instruction in the doctrines of the various schools of psychology than in its religious heritage, but often one could discover in these preoccupations the same assurance that conformity with its instructions was the way to wholeness if not to holiness.

Servanthood in the World

Moral discipline, personal ethics (already something more than religiosity) plays an important role in the Christian life. But not for the sake of righteousness. God has already taken care of that. The Christian life is a consequence of the new being, a rebirth to new possibilities. Moral discipline comes out of my new freedom and my consequent commitment and enablement to do the will of God, to be his deputy in the world. Christian sainthood, even with all its imperfections, is not a matter of moral exercises; it is the practice of servanthood in the world. It is the care of God's children, God's creatures, God's creation; it is the freely given commitment to live for others, as Christ lived for others.

How shall I serve my neighbor?

The opportunities are manifold, and the human situations are varied. I must set my own priorities, and I must act within my individual circumstances. Surely marriage and parenthood offer one kind of opportunity. This may be the apparently most personal and also the most universal. It is one on which the religious groups have expended a great deal of energy, to which they have given much attention. Sometimes indeed to the extent that the home has seemed for some the refuge from all other responsibility; we have become guilty at times of a domestic *incurvatus in se*. Sexual ecstasy is not a surrogate of righteousness, no matter how right and important it may be in its appropriate place. Here too a psychological analog of pietism has often seduced Christians into self-centeredness again. Fortunately women's liberation, perhaps unconsciously, has called many of us away from some of our domestic idolatry.

We can serve the neighbor elsewhere — at work, at play, and in politics. Not all of us are called to political activity; not all of us have gifts for political leadership. But too many of us have failed to see that one very important way of helping people, of serving the neighbor, is through concern for the affairs of our community, local, state or province, and national. In politics love of neighbor can express itself both personally and institutionally: politics offers opportunities for compassionate sensitivity to the neighbor's need and challenges its practitioners to make the structures of society serve the cause of justice more adequately. By joining with others the Christian can strengthen his efforts through corporate witness.

While this corporate witness can take a number of forms, particularly through participation in a variety of secular organizations, the one form recently under fire has been the corporate witness of organized religious groups. Here too misunderstandings have their roots in traditions we have inherited. We need first of all to get some clarity on what organized religious groups are and what they are not.

Organized religious groups, identifiable generally as corporations not for profit with boards of trustees, officers, headquarters buildings, staffs, and all the other paraphernalia necessary for carrying on their affairs are empirical exemplars of "the one holy catholic and apostolic church"; *they are not identical with it.* They represent organized manifestations of the people of God in a variety of historical appearances. For any of them to appropriate the title "the church" for themselves is an arrogant claim. Many of them make just such a claim. But from the point of view of this study each is seen as a particular empirical fraction (by no means pure) of the total company of Christians in the world.

Each such group has, of course, its own understanding of the traditions of the people of God, their teachings and their commitments. Each strives through a particular pattern of organization to give actuality to a vision of what the body of Christ can, is, and ought to be. All of these groups struggle in various ways with the problems of hierarchy (in various guises and disguises) and collegiality (encouraged, discouraged, often ignored). From our viewpoint all represent trajectories, sometimes intersecting, at other times parallel, of the pilgrimage of the people of God through history.

Two patterns have dominated the ways in which these

groups have handled their expressions of the body of Christ. One is to identify one little fraction as the organized sum total of the "one holy catholic and apostolic church." These are the true believers, the chosen of God. Outside of this company no one belongs among the saved — except by the grace of God (which is the way I thought all of us were to get in). More than one group, including some very small ones, have made this claim. We have them in considerable numbers in this country; other countries have them too.

We tend to discount these claims; they are very difficult to take seriously. Thus the second option is more tempting. The true church of God is invisible. Thus we need not really bother with organizational and institutional realities. "Where two or three are gathered," there the church is present. What counts is individual faith, individual commitment, individual freedom. No organization ought to violate any conscience, ought to press demands upon me in my daily conduct of affairs. I will settle my course of action in communion with the Lord.

The convenience of both of these approaches is the ease with which they ignore the dialectical tensions of the Christian life. Adherents of the claim that theirs is the true church have always had difficulty not only with outsiders but also with keeping their own household in doctrinal and moral order. Exclusivism and self-righteousness frequently keep company, indeed are probably common-law bed partners. The chief sin may lie in the claims the organization makes about itself, i.e., the *simul* is almost impossible to accept. The other camp, the individualist Christians, find themselves hard pushed to develop any sense of moral discipline beyond a few matters of personal ethics that are often more reflective of their cultural situation than of faith and its commitments. If the "true church" often becomes a culturally irrelevant little enclave of persons with peculiar habits and/or peculiar beliefs, the other Christians succumb too easily to becoming simply mirrors of the prejudices and preoccupations of their socio-economic class, race or national situation in life. Lacking dialectical tension, they fail to understand the uneasy conscience that the *simul* requires.

Christian commitment requires some kind of visibility. The people of God are gathered in empirical organizations through which they give embodiment to their loyalties. The "one holy catholic and apostolic church" exists in, with, and under the myriad of existing ecclesiastical organizations. At times its visibility may be barely noticeable under the overwhelming burden of its social environment; at all times the visibility is imperfect, partial, under the judgment of the *simul*. Every empirical organization stands under the mandate to measure up to what it should be. None can have an easy conscience; none can claim to be "the church."

Thus each such organization must recognize that it can bind only by persuasion, not by coercion. How and where it draws the line against specific individual Christians cannot be automatically determined. But at the same time as an empirical visible witness to the fact that "one holy catholic and apostolic church" does exist on earth, every empirical organization must bear collective testimony to its existence. Witness is inescapable.

Witness is inescapable because there must be public ministry, public proclamation. Without the preaching of the gospel the people of God cannot be gathered. In the preaching the church, the body of Christ, becomes visible, no matter how imperfectly. At the same time such preaching must be genuinely public; it must reach out to "the world," the audience for whom the gospel is intended. To restrict the Word to a private gathering on Sunday morning, no matter how solemn the surroundings, to keep it as the carefully guarded treasure of a secret elite, is to deny the mandate of the Lord.

The Word of God is both law and gospel. Justice is also part of God's agenda. Thus by some means, whether from the pulpit, through the recommendations of commissions, the resolutions of assemblies, the actions of administrators, the Word must become public. The demand for justice must be heard.

3

THE NATURE OF CORPORATE WITNESS

As a corporate body every empirical organization of the people of God has the means to do certain jobs; it has the machinery for making decisions. Through an elected presiding officer, through an executive board, as well as through a representative assembly, it can act as a corporate body. A synod in convention speaks as a corporate body; it has the machinery, good or bad, to determine the contents of its witness.

When a religious organization as a corporate body acts, it may be addressing its own members, agencies, institutions, or organizations; or it may be addressing those outside its membership, collectively or individually. Every such action is a kind of witness; an expression, however imperfect, of the faith. Our judgments — even before we deal with questions of the expediency or inexpediency of a particular action — must deal with the action as witness. That we have so often failed to make just this kind of judgment is a measure of the failures in our understanding of the collective reality of the people of God.

The witness of a corporate body is not, of course, equivalent to the opinions of all its individual members; sometimes it may not even represent very many. Nevertheless the witness remains the legitimate voice of the body which issued the message. That message cannot be imposed upon those who dissent;

they should, however, take it seriously as a witness coming from an organized expression of the people of God, from that organized expression to which they have themselves pledged loyalty. No one who dissents should dissent on frivolous or irrelevant grounds. But at the same time the organization must not coerce; it can and must ask all the members to reflect seriously on the witness being made.

What is involved at this point is a critical interplay of authority and freedom. The authority invoked, however, is not merely the empirical strength and prestige of the corporate religious body. The authority at issue is the authority of the Word of God. But that authority does not come to the members in disembodied form. The proclamation of that Word with authority is the task of the public ministry. The church has a ministry in order that the Word be made public. The people of God are under the mandate to proclaim the gospel *to the world, in the world*. The persons we know as "the clergy" exist in order that this public proclamation may occur, and that through this public proclamation and through the celebration of those gathered through that proclamation, the people of God may be rendered visible. To be rendered visible, to be proclaimed as authority, means nothing less than to make a claim upon the obedience of all who hear. Thus public ministry gives structure, embodiment, visibility, order to the people of God. In this way, the principle of hierarchy works itself out in witness. The public ministry has a claim upon the people of God even, indeed precisely, when what is proclaimed runs counter to what the large majority of the devout understand as Christian.

But this is only half the story. For the proclamation of the Word gathers a company of believers; the Word bears fruit as it calls into being those who are called to be the servants of their neighbors, called to the freedom of serving on God's behalf, as his deputies — using Bonhoeffer's remarkable word — and in the company of these and only in their company can the authority of the Word be properly exercised. All those whom the Word calls and gathers are also custodians of the

Word. Consequently there must be lively encounter between the whole company of believers and those called to public servanthood. For the public servant exercises his authority only in and through the whole company of believers. He is accountable to them, just as they are called upon to listen to him. It is in, with, and under these human forms that both hierarchy and collegiality exist under the authority of the Word.

There is no room here then for a democratic sentimentality that absolutizes the will of the majority; nor is there any place for the romantic adulation of hierarchy. They function rather as mutal correctives to the temptations of coercive authority or chaotic freedom.

Forms of Corporate Witness

How then shall we witness corporately?

We begin with witness to ourselves. For the authority of the Word on any question must first be addressed to those who accept that authority. The clergy as the teachers of the faithful dare not be silent wherever human need, human injustice, human sinfulness whether in collective or individual form abound.

One of the great failures of the organized religious groups of our day, particularly among Protestants, has been the failure of the teaching function. The defect was moral and intellectual; it was in our theological understanding and in our ethical instructions.

The literature of Christian ethics in the nineteenth and earlier twentieth century to a large degree is a literature of pious preoccupation with self; the goal of the Christian life became my own growth in Christian virtue, shaping my own personality. Care for the neighbor, in so far as it received a place in the textbooks of Christian ethics, came under the rubric of developing habits of charity and compassion. Concern for the welfare of others became a small part of the private expression of what it meant to be Christian.

Social concern became a matter of benevolence not of justice. Thus a vulgar corruption of the two kingdom notion
became a Protestant stock in trade. As recently as 1960 an
editorial in *Christianity Today* insisted that "When the
Church seeks to infuse the government's ministry of justice
(tax-supported) with its religious witness (benevolent voluntar-
ism), it destroys the distinction between justice and benevolence." All awareness of dialectical tension is here lost;
apparently justice is not something with which an organized
religious group should be concerned. Nor should the state
respond to human needs except on the basis of rights. This
would rule out not only many forms of organized public
welfare but most assuredly disaster relief, which surely rests
more on spontaneous response to suffering than to established
legal rights to rehabilitation at public expense.

This older understanding of the Christian life can only be
called a betrayal of the Reformation. Whatever justifications
may be made for this shift in emphasis — we can offer historical explanations of how the shift came about — we must be
honest in seeing that this understanding fundamentally sepa-
rates what the Reformers had kept together, love and justice,
personhood and official duty.

The initial teaching task which all of us must undertake
is to recover the fundamental insight into the sweeping scope
of my obligation to my neighbor, to recover the vision of
social justice as an integral part of the Christian proclamation.

The authority of the Word must be re-asserted in all its
comprehensiveness. But it must not be asserted coercively.
We do not need a new generation of priestly tyrants thun-
dering from Protestant pulpits to a submissive people. Not
only does such an approach hold little promise of success, but
it deserves to fail, because it does not take seriously the priesthood of believers. More precisely, the teaching of the clergy
must be set in a context of conversation, of persuasion, of
reciprocal correction and mutual encouragement, because in
the freedom of the gospel each believer must in his particular

places of opportunity translate the witness in personal terms. Witness is not a matter of lip service; it is the ways in which you and I concretely go about achieving justice in the communities and within the organizations to which we belong.

A particular case in point is what happened in the churches on the question of race relations. I know I could rehearse many sins of omission in our corporate existence before 1954. After 1956, when the denomination to which I belong, then known as the United Lutheran Church in America, made a collective decision to support school desegregation, almost nothing happened in terms of the kinds of teaching I have just been talking about. I do not mean that there were no programs, no pronouncements, no prodding. These obviously occurred.

But suppose there had been at that time, despite all the difficulties, all the resistance, a genuine effort — backed with an adequate budget and organizational know-how — to help every congregation and all of its members, regardless of where on the spectrum of opinion the congregation, its pastor, or people might be, to undertake a serious study of the Scriptures, of the basic teachings of the church, of our understanding of ourselves as Christians on this particular question. Such a self-examination would have required great patience, great forebearance, tremendous skills in dealing with human emotions. It would have required a different understanding of the teaching responsibilities of the clergy, indeed of our religious organization itself.

Something even more important would have been required and still is required. The teachers, the administrators, the pastors — in other words, the persons vested with authority in the hierarchy — would have been required to give concrete embodiment to the universal priesthood of believers. To trust in the universal priesthood means to believe that individual believers scattered over thousands of congregations would in fact respond affirmatively to the authority of the Word. If what we resolved after 1954 indeed expressed the teachings of the Word of God, then the Word should also convince the honest and sincere Christian believer coming to that Word with an open mind and heart. The truth is that we did not give the power of the Word full opportunity to operate. Our practice denied our affirmation of the universal priesthood.

We need to recognize a twofold failure. We had no effective witness to ourselves. Almost twenty years after the beginning of the Civil Rights Revolution of our day a large number of Christian congregations in all denominations have probably never directly faced the question of the nature of church membership. For surely the first word of the church on the question of race should have been to lay on the consciences of all church members the apostolic witness, "There is neither Jew nor Greek, male nor female, bond nor free." This would have been a difficult witness, doubly difficult because on this question the church would have been dealing with the question of its own nature, not with issues of domestic politics.

This is not a plea for some kind of total democracy in the congregations. It is a plea for the exercise of collegiality under the authority of the Word; it is a plea for a responsible hierarchy responsive to the entire company of believers under the authority of the Word. It is a hope and a prayer that we may take seriously the organizational imperatives in the dialectic of priesthood and public ministry, freedom and order, collegiality and hierarchy.

It is also a recognition, let this be emphasized, that the creditability of all Christian churches, certainly of those who proclaim their faithful witness on the question of race, must be seriously questioned so long as these churches have not faced the question of their own segregated condition. Not having put our own house in order, could we really expect others, blacks in particular, to believe we were serious about housing and school segregation. Our own church-related colleges too often lagged far behind public institutions in their practices. On the other hand, suppose as many as twenty percent of local white congregations had effectively struggled to a new understanding of what it means to be faithful to the gospel. What kind of witness under such circumstances would laity and clergy together have been able to bring to the larger community?

I do not want to underestimate the difficulties attendant on such a course of action. It involves a recognition that effective wrestling with the problems of white racism is in fact a problem *for white people first of all;* more specifically, that it is a priority item on the agenda of white Christians. It remains to this day a priority item, because it is a piece of unfinished business for the vast majority of white American Christian congregations. The politicians have in fact on the whole done a better job than the pious.

To call for this kind of public witness is not a question of justice, of social action; *what is at stake is simply fidelity to the gospel,* simple recognition that in Jesus Christ we are in fact all brothers and sisters, that the first place where the dividing wall must collapse in our day — as in the first century — is in the company of believers. This has not yet happened. It must happen.

Fidelity to the gospel here takes the form of a commitment to social justice. Only by a recovery of the biblical meaning of reconciliation and commitment, as Preston Williams has recently pointed out, will we begin to discover the power to bring down the barriers. Only then will we discover how to right the wrongs that have been so repeatedly committed.

Thus Christian political ethics must begin within the believing community; it must begin with faithfulness to the gospel. The first witness of a corporate religious group must be its witness to itself.

Let me continue the exploration of our corporate witness to ourselves with a brief exposition of two other forms of action. Almost inseparable from teaching yet different from it is pastoral care. As Christians encounter the ambiguities of acting in accordance with justice in the larger community, they will not infrequently be in need of a listening ear. What better place for listening can we name than the community of believers, especially those trained to provide care and counsel when we encounter cases of conscience.

Pastoral care in its traditional sense encompasses a great deal more than binding up the emotional wounds of an individual; it is much more than acceptance. Indeed we have forgotten too easily that salvation has something to do with wholeness, that more than forgiveness is integral to a faithful Christian life. Whether we must bind up the wounds that come from a broken marriage or deal with the struggles of the Christian employer seeking to meet the demands of equal employment opportunities, pastoral care must concern itself with justice as well as love, with correction as well as forgiveness. We have learned new ways to deal with human beings; doctrinaire imposition of our opinions is often the worst instrument of justice. But a presumed sensitivity to another which allows that person to persist in wrong-doing, in injustice, is moral cowardice; it is as grievous a fault in a pastor as a surgeon's refusal to operate because he may inflict pain upon the patient.

In dealing with "the person" in psychological terms, while failing to deal with social responsibilities and relationships, we have not only trivialized the gospel into private therapy; we have betrayed it. We are practicing a "psychological pietism" as one-sided as the old legalistic pietism.

Finally every corporate organization of Christian believers must be an exemplary community. Quite bluntly, we did very little about demands for equal opportunity in employment or education, to take just two facets of our corporate life, in the administrative offices, the boards and commissions, the agencies and institutions of our religious denominations, until years after many of these pressures had become matters of law in the larger community. Our example denied our claims; we were not creditable in the public arena.

Political Witness

Having said all this with respect to witness to ourselves, we have only made a beginning. Because the place of witness for social justice is the larger community. The primary agency for that witness is the political structure of our society.

How do we witness corporately?

We witness, first of all, through our recognition that while every segment of human activity stands under God and therefore under the demand for justice, a great many of our fellow citizens will not recognize any claim couched in religious language. If we would have them listen, we must speak to them in their own language.

This means that in the public arena, when we are addressing the general public, we speak in the language of justice; we come with the arguments of reason and experience.

Our basic conviction of the worth and dignity of every human being rests ultimately upon the simple affirmation of faith that Jesus Christ died for all. God intends all his children to be free. Within the framework of our commitment to freedom and equality, we can say a great deal about justice to the members of our society.

Our corporate witness for justice is both priestly and prophetic. Our witness is priestly because we recognize that human institutions have a legitimate claim upon the obedience of citizens. The call for law and order has its place in the witness of the Christian community, but we must be careful that we are not using such a call to cover up vested interests, to draw attention away from injustice and oppression.

Our witness is prophetic when it calls for changes in social arrangements, when we seek reform of the status quo, when we go against the grain of established custom and community habits. In faithfulness to the Word, prophetic witness is a continuing necessity in our corporate life; indeed prophetic witness must be present in any human society short of the kingdom of God itself. To deny corporate witness is implicitly to claim a greater righteousness for a social order than actually exists.

Corporate witness is more than a matter of resolutions or recommendations. In a social order as complex as our own, even where social evils may be glaringly apparent, corporate witness demands thorough study and analysis. On the national level, frequently also on regional and state levels, our main line Christian communions have done fairly well with this requirement. We have, with some notable exceptions, done poorly at the level where most of the people are — at the level of the congregation. That is to say, we have done fairly well with the leadership, particularly the clergy, but we have done little with the general membership.

How crucial this difference in what we do at different levels is will vary with the particular issue, with different groups, perhaps even with different regions, but in most instances it is very crucial. We have in this country, for example, a welfare system which is functioning very poorly, a system that tends to pauperize people, to destroy their independence and self-respect rather than to help them to more self-sustaining roles in their communities. The weaknesses of the welfare structure have long been apparent to many professionals, including many of the professional welfare workers in the Christian denominations. Yet the basic attitudes towards welfare in the general public work for the most part to perpetuate the malfunctioning system that now exists.

We have had official ecclesiastical pronouncements on this issue. Our welfare professionals have testified in Washington and in the state capitals. Yet very few pastors have had an opportunity to become familiar with the criticisms and the counter-proposals; almost none of the laity. Thus we have undermined the effectiveness of our own prophetic voice. We have not instructed the consciences of the believers; we have not engaged in conversation with the pew; we have not listened to questions, heard rebuttals, taken opposition seriously.

Corporate witness is more than an impersonal analysis of issues; it is at the same time a concern for the personal situation of all involved in a social crisis. I believe the prison troubles at Attica, New York, were a serious indictment of the failures of our correctional system, failures in which we all share. Saying this and criticizing certain aspects of the way in which New York authorities handled that situation does not, however, mean that we forget the human torment, the struggles of conscientious decision-making, of the warden of that prison. Some of that struggle came through even on the impersonal medium of television. Prophetic witness needs the dimension of personal concern; the enemy is also to be loved and comforted.

The transition from corporate to individual witness is not really difficult. The demand rests upon all of us in every social role to be concerned for personhood, for freedom, for the welfare of our neighbors. We are all called upon to perform our duties faithfully, that is, to work in all our worldly tasks in the fullness of faith.

The difficulty in corporate witness, as in individual witness, does not lie in the general injunction to act in behalf of justice. It lies rather in the discovery of justice. For the answers are not always obvious. Disagreements are in fact the order of the day.

This is not the place nor the time to enter into the analysis of specific situations. We can, however, look at some of the general obstacles we shall encounter. I shall choose them from the realm of politics.

The chief temptation to which all of us are subject is that of confusing our vested interests with justice. This is why Luther tells us that in our own cases we should be willing to suffer injustice patiently rather than demand justice for ourselves. This injunction applies as much to organized groups, including the church, as it does to individuals. Reinhold Niebuhr years ago pointed out the particular dilemma in dealing with organized selfishness. We shall deal with this again.

Most problems cannot be handled by some simple exercise of self-denial. For my interests and my neighbor's needs generally get well entangled with one another. Tax reform may indeed be what justice requires for the welfare of many families; can I deny I may also benefit?

The more subtle problem, however, is not open individual selfishness. We will always have outspoken critics who will challenge us at this point. Very few public officials can any longer gets away with a blatantly self-serving kind of public career. But all of us have been indoctrinated from childhood on with the perspectives of a particular social class; we view the world, for the most part unconsciously, through well established biases. The strongest of these we even identify with the natural order of the world, given beyond our control. An American audience need not be reminded how much of our thinking about questions of race took this form. In some ways these unconscious distortions were even worse in the North than in the South, because we believed ourselves free of them.

In some ways then I cannot help seeing the world as a middle class white male Protestant of the generation over fifty. But in some ways I can help it. For my first task in personal and social relationships is self-examination. In the explanation of Baptism in the Small Catechism, Luther calls for daily contrition. That call remains both valid and necessary.

Daily contrition is rarely self-generated. We need our critics. We need above all our radical critics. We must listen to them, especially to their accusations. But we must go beyond contrition. Confession may be good for the soul, as the proverb has it, but the body politic usually needs remedial action.

The first step in such remedial action is the acceptance of personal responsibility. Perhaps the greatest good that effective preaching on social issues could accomplish is not the delineation of programs of social reform from the pulpit, but simply convincing the devout that they have a personal responsibility. The preacher must address me in all my roles, not just as father, friend, fellow believer, but as citizen, office holder, a person with power. The pulpit must call me to accountability, but without violating my personal judgment as a member of the community of faith.

To accept personal responsibility is to know that I can do something about questions of racial injustice, poverty, pollution, war, tax reform, and so on. I may very well not have any ultimate solutions. Indeed I usually use my lack of ultimate solutions as an excuse for not doing anything.

What can I do? There are no easy ways to spell out the concrete mandates for compassionate sensitivity and social justice. The agenda may differ from community to community; the opportunities may differ from Christian to Christian.

But we do not completely lack signposts. The civil use of the law, as Luther reminds us, exists for the restraint of evil-doers. More generally the moral order to which Romans 13 refers, the order which is God's will for justice, the supreme authority to which every person is to be subject, works to interdict evil and to support good. That is, the very nature of the world as Christians understand it works in the direction of justice; not automatically, but through human action. We can therefore apply reason and experience to discover what kind of social order does in fact make for freedom and justice. In this quest the old imperatives about killing, truth-telling, stealing, and marital fidelity seem to point directions in which good order is to be found. We shall explore some of the implications of this in a later chapter.

4

THE FAILURE OF
CORPORATE WITNESS

To be concerned for social justice, to be compassionate, requires not only committed action; it requires organized action. Pious resolutions do not bind up wounds, feed the hungry, or provide a shelter for the homeless. Commitment can only be rendered effective through organization.

We must distinguish two facets of involvement: the participation of individual pastors of congregations in protest movements, marches, demonstrations, sit-ins, in which the question of the propriety of the individual person's action in the context of the public role of a pastor is central; and, the role which specific voluntary protest organizations played in using a Christian ethic as the basis for legitimizing actions challenging existing policy and social arrangements. Our primary concern here is with the second.

Neither the civil rights movement nor the protest against the Vietnam war were primarily denominationally organized efforts for social change, although some denominational staff and leaders gave public support. Indeed the number of organized *denominational* efforts that involved explicit planning for social change is minimal. Organized religious support moved to a climax in the period following the Birmingham demonstrations of 1963 through the Civil Rights battle in the Senate in 1964. Then the support broke apart under the impact of the Black Manifesto and the rise of Black Power. During the time of extensive support the money and manpower came primarily from a limited number of denominations; even among these the contributions represented only a small fraction of their total budgets. Except in the instances of support for legislative efforts in the Senate during 1964 and the funds contributed for community organization purposes, these expenditures cannot be considered as contributing to efforts to change the basic structure of American society in any meaningful way.

Thus, contrary to popular belief the mainline religious groups did relatively little in fostering major social changes, at least in terms of the percentages of total budgets committed or the proportion of personnel devoted to activities of this kind. Yet they appeared highly involved. What was done had a high degree of visibility; furthermore, the working press, including those responsible for newscasting have little knowledge of the structures of responsibility and accountability in the denominations. The Southern Christian Leadership Conference, for example, although quite clearly an organization based on the specific religious beliefs and precepts of its leaders, is not—and never claimed to be—a "church." Nor could Clergy and Laity Concerned about Vietnam be identified in this way. The spokesmen of these groups did not speak as representatives of the National Baptist Convention, the United Presbyterian Church in the United States of America, the Archdiocese of New York, the Lutheran Church in America, or, for that matter, St. Johns-by-the-Gas-Station.

The press and newscasters identified the leaders and spokesmen as clergy, as religious functionaries; they identified their organizations as religious organizations. Great numbers of newspaper readers and television viewers drew their inferences, and the identification was complete.

The Churches and Civil Rights

With respect to the civil rights struggle, the identification was not completely erroneous. The leadership of the major denominations gave a considerable measure of support to facets of the struggle, although the support varied a great deal from group to group, issue to issue, and from one phase of the struggle to the next. Had the commitment of the mainline white Protestant groups been anywhere as monolithic as some popular sources assumed, Martin Luther King's "Letter from Birmingham Jail" would have made little sense.

A more significant role in support of social change, particularly during the middle phase of the civil rights movement, can be attributed to the National Council of Churches. During the early 1960s the strategy of involvement on the part of the National Council changed in an important way. Both the change and the reasons why it occurred are significant; it is equally important to note that except for one program area, the change in strategy was not sustained.

The National Council of Churches is neither a super-church nor an agency with autonomous powers; the member denominations have always been careful in the delegation of initiative. For the most part the National Council provides services of various kinds to its members. The strongest support for its work has come from a small number of mainline churches which have developed commitments to action programs aimed at social change (United Presbyterians, United Methodists, United Church of Christ, Episcopalians, and Lutheran Church in America). In addition, an important supporting constituency for National Council policy exists in the professional staffs of state and local councils of churches. Over the years the selective processes at work in staffing the National Council professional level positions resulted in a disproportionate number of persons whose education occurred in a small number of interdenominational seminaries where the leading teachers of social ethics were also active. These persons may be seen as a kind of "professional elite" in the ecclesiastical structure of American conciliar Protestantism.

In the 1960s concern with the problems of race in particular shifted from education to action. The initiative did not come from the conciliar professionals; black leadership from Martin

Luther King, Jr. to the student activisits began a campaign of demonstrations, sit-ins, and other forms of protest activity that grew into a major social movement, heralding a new militancy in the search for racial justice.

At this critical juncture for a short period of time the National Council brought into being its Commission on Race and Religion (CORR) as an agency for social justice authorized "to make commitments, call for action, take risks in behalf of the National Council of Churches which are required by the situation . . ." The immediate occasion for this action was the nationally publicized confrontation in Birmingham, including the imprisonment of Martin Luther King, Jr. For a period of about four years, during which significant support was generated for civil rights legislation, including the breaking of a Senate filibuster, the National Council provided important leadership. Especially through the agency of its state and local councils it was able to mobilize clergy and denominational support in bringing pressures to bear in Washington. These years may be seen as the phase of interracial cooperation, good feeling, and optimism in the civil rights struggle. By the summer of 1967, however, the functions of CORR were returned to a more normal bureaucratic niche in the Office of Religion and Race within a new Department of Social Justice; at the same time many of the key persons left National Council employment. Although the rhetoric continued, the period of effective action had passed.

A second highly significant development occurred—in the arena of community organization. Ghetto residents in certain northern metropolitan centers were engaged in direct battles with local power structures. An important independent agency to provide continuing support and overall planning, the Interreligious Foundation for Community Organization (IFCO) came into being. IFCO is administratively totally independent of both the National Council and the individual religious denominations who contribute to its programs. It is under effective black control. In many ways IFCO represents the continuation of the religious support of the Alinsky style in community organization; more important, however, is the achievement of self-determination in the program of organizing minority peoples for action in their own behalf. As a department of the National Council IFCO would probably not have achieved either its level of funding nor its present level of effectiveness. Equally important, with the creation of IFCO the sometimes heated debate within the denominations over question of community organization styles has largely disappeared; the work is no longer as highly visible; it gets much less attention from the same media that once played up the battle against Kodak in Rochester or the hearings on the activities of the Blackstone Rangers. While the accomplishments of IFCO remain modest measured against the task, it has nevertheless contributed significantly to the creation of self-help organizations in minority communities.

In noting the degree to which National Council action was the work of a professional elite and not representative of the memberships of the religious groups as a whole, we must add two comments. Given the limited investment most National Council membership had in the Council, finding program services of greater value than social policy, we should not be surprised that the initiative lay with a relatively small group. But the resistance to this leadership which developed rather rapidly (reflecting not only the fears of many white Christians but also the fact that black leadership was getting at central questions of power and privilege) shows that the early emphasis on education for social reform had not in fact been very effective. Had the educational work been done—as it was done in certain leadership cadres—more support would have been forthcoming. Contrary to popular beliefs about continued National Council pressures for change, after 1967 a strategic withdrawal actually occurred. In addition, for reasons related to the struggles of the 1960s, a great deal of National Council energy went into structural reorganization.

A further dimension of the religious involvement of the 1960s needs to be examined. The use of organizations other than official denominational groups themselves probably helped account for the effectiveness of both the civil rights and the anti-Vietnam war movements. The fact that these organizations had gathered together committed persons across denominational lines, that they were not beholden to religious bureaucracies for program approval, money, and personnel, that they did not have to deal with a whole host of other issues on their agendas, gave them strategic flexibility, clarity of direction, and consequently an effectiveness the denominations could not have achieved.

Since in some measure the leadership of the mainline denominations, including the leadership of the National Council of Churches, generally supported the goals and programs of these movements, since in addition official gatherings of the organized religious groups were called upon to pass resolutions of support, vote funds for certain related programs, and in the instance of civil rights open up the agencies, institutions, and congregations of the religious groups to improved practices in recruitment, employment, and services, an arena also existed within the religious organizations for the battle to be joined. One could not deal directly with SCLC, SNCC, CORE, or the anti-war groups, but one could find an arena to challenge those who gave support and religious legitimacy.

The Question of Legitimacy

The real issue in social action must be seen as legitimacy. As already indicated, except in the last phases of the civil rights struggle, the amount of money, personnel, or time involved was small. Most of the involvement came at the national staff level, not at the regional, state, or local community level. Yet quite strikingly the question of legitimacy became harder to deal with the closer one came to the locus where change was to occur.

The debate over the legitimacy of social action revealed serious defects in the procedures that had developed in the mainline religious groups in dealing with questions of social action. The personnel responsible for social education and action in the major groups were in frequent contact with one another, not only because they worked out of offices located in New York City, but because they regularly represented their denominations at meetings of the related National Council Departments and Commissions, sometimes also at General Board meetings; in brief, they were continually re-inforcing their own perceptions of particular social problems. The resistance directed to them came from "outsiders," not from within the circle. Since representatives of denominations less inclined to support social action tended to be lax in attending National Council meetings, one can understand why it must have seemed reasonable to misread opposition, whose noisiest leadership came from reactionary spokesmen from outside the National Council or the supporting denominational leadership; the religious leaders did not see the opposition as representative of what the majority of church members believed. Furthermore, as a perusal of the literature of the early 1960s will indicate, discussions of social action paid almost no attention to the questions of popular participation. Hierarchical leadership went unchallenged.

Even at representative gatherings of church bodies the records show that little internal opposition was voiced in the early years. Moral sympathies clearly lay with oppressed blacks; the Vietnam War did not become a big issue until the second half of the Johnson administration. Lay delegates to representative ecclesiastical gatherings probably over-represent the more sensitive persons in local churches; at the same time, these representatives—not unlike the rank and file at other gatherings—tend to vote for what seem to be the administration measures. Thus, despite the fact that by and large the social action personnel had devoted little attention to mobilizing the people in local congregations in support of particular issues, the support was apparently there. Large voting majorities at national and even at state gatherings were taken to provide sufficient legitimation and motivation for membership support. But the votes of representative assemblies turned out to be poor clues to the states of opinions in the constituencies.

It was one matter entirely to react viscerally to the behavior of "Bull" Connor in the Birmingham confrontations; it became another matter when James Forman presented his demands for reparations. A basis for the legitimacy of the involvement of religious groups in political action had not actually been developed to any effective degree.

Legitimacy was assumed to be identical with a majority decision made at a national, state, or regional gathering, or in some instances, with the resolutions or position papers of authorized commissions, boards, or staff officials. The theological rationales underlying these decisions were accepted as adequate, consistent with the doctrinal traditions of the religious groups, and authoritative. Thus denominational leaders did not recognize how serious the problem of legitimacy was.

The disagreement had two facets. When the rhetoric of social action changed from "justice" to "power," from serving victims of oppression to supporting revolutionary movements, the supporting base disappeared. The working theologies of many Christians, parish pastors as well as lay persons, provided clear support for a vision of a "just society," in which every one received fair treatment; an "egalitarian society," particularly in the distribution of political power, demanded a different image, for which conventional theology and ethical discourse had not prepared church members.

In the years after World War II the leadership of the major religious bodies changed appreciably. Professional staff increased in number; elected leaders became full-time administrators and often acquired assistants. The new elite, many of whom shared the advantage of graduate education, were oriented to a bureaucratic career and took their cues for policy and theological reflection from a strikingly different context from the one in which parish pastors and rank and file members were at work. The result of these developments, under conditions of administrative centralization, with the main thrust of the flow of communications from the top downwards, could only be a mutual insensitivity and often increasing mistrust.

The problems that came in the 1960s had their roots in the late 1940s. The baby boom, shifts in where people lived, and rising consumer expectations, brought far-reaching changes. During the heyday of mission activity few denominational executives reflected on the kinds of problems that were in gestation. Large numbers of middle Americans moved to the suburbs, contributing to the development of the white noose around increasing black central cities. An honest analysis must see these changes as partly the outcome of the housing policies which the New Deal had espoused (FHA in particular). These policies contributed heavily to the urban crisis, notably to the breakdown of urban schools. But many liberals, within and without the churches, rarely questioned these basic policies.

Ecclesiastical Imperialism

A more serious ideological shortcoming also helped misdirect religious responses. Many sectors of American Protestantism had developed a deep-seated ecclesiastical imperialism. In part an outcome of the development of competitive denominationalism as the basic structural pattern for American religion, ecclesiastical imperialism stimulated the churches to develop a series of satellite dependencies, to which both by sentiment and budget allocation, the denominations were heavily committed. In many ways these expressed particular denominational identities, were ways of mobilizing the loyalty of the rank and file, even though one might be hard put to discover genuinely unique defining characteristics. Thus it was the mark of mature denominational development to have a number of "church-related" colleges, welfare agencies, hospitals, and other institutions through which the denomination provided a variety of programs not only to its own constituencies but also to other groups, including the poor. Behind the ecclesiastical imperialism lay a state of mind that defined a program, an organization, or an institution as essentially religious only if an explicit church relationship or sponsorship existed.

The major religious groups had thus invested heavily in past forms of corporate Christian action. In the 1950s and 1960s these satellite programs themselves underwent considerable physical and financial expansion. When the social conflicts arose, denominational leaders often found that the maintenance of existing structures and denominational unity had a price, namely, resistance to open discussion of new issues and denial of all but token energy or funding to new initiatives. Leaders appealed to the strategy of consensus, satisfying neither their conservative constituents nor the new radicals.

As the issues sharpened, adherents of both the left and the right became disenchanted with their leadership. On the one hand, many church-goers felt that leaders were not sharing with them the extent of their commitment to social change, that the ordinary member was indeed increasingly powerless to determine what was being done with his money and in his name. At the same time, those more radically inclined, including many of the young, felt that leadership was more interested in institutional stability and survival than in effective social change. The tide of youth protest, heavily influenced by the role which young people played in anti-Vietnam demonstrations, overlapped with the period in which the leadership came increasingly under attack for its initiative on racial questions; the reluctance of institutional leaders to move with greater clarity and conviction quickly turned off many of the young. For many persons heavily involved at either extreme in the polarizations which were taking place, "staying together" was of lesser importance than confronting the issues. In some instances, in fact, the inability of moderates to define a clear-cut choice may itself have contributed to their defeat.

The ideology of consensus ran into severe theological storms. At issue was the degree of ecclesiological warrant to be attached to the pronouncements of religious assemblies, especially official actions. Presumably formally approved resolutions carry some theological weight. This seems a simple enough principle. But by no stretch of the imagination can the annual or biennial assemblies of American religious groups (or of similar denominational gatherings elsewhere) be equated with the early ecumenical councils (the exact status of some of these can also be questioned). A good many of the items on the agendas of such assemblies are housekeeping matters dealing with the reception of reports, organizational problems, and budgets. How does one single out among the variety of policy declarations those which have some special doctrinal or ethical status? What is this status?

Obviously a complex motion changing the pension arrangements for the clergy and a motion on racial justice are different matters. They may occupy equal amounts of time on the agenda, lead to parliamentary maneuvering on the part of advocates or opponents, and finally receive similar majorities. But what are the implications in terms of of commitment? Ironically the bureaucratic machinery of a religious group can usually conform the practice of the group to new pension requirements more quickly than it can win acceptance of a policy of racial justice. Laying aside this consideration, however, we must recognize that the question of the official authority inherent in policy declarations on controversial issues has no settled answer; the ideology of consensus may lead many to the assumption that what is voted automatically requires consent. But in what sense and on what authority can the vote of an ecclesiastical assembly be given doctrinal status and made binding upon the church member's conscience? If one rejects, as I think one must, any identification of an empirical religious organization with "the church," what mandate do ecclesiastical pronouncements possess? Does majority vote determine doctrine?

While liberal church leaders would of course shy away from any assertion giving the pronouncements of religious assemblies the character of dogma, their emotional commitments often lead them to make sweeping claims. The relationship between the gospel and social justice seems patent; thus when truth is self-evident, the apparent issue is not the dogmatism of the protagonist but the bigotry of the antagonist. But the road from the universal claims of the gospel, e.g., about the brotherhood and sisterhood of all people, to specific conclusions or to specific action programs does not in fact seem obvious to many church members. In part this is without question a tragic commentary on the shortcomings of Christian understanding; certainly it reflects the failure to instruct, noted above. But it is also true that no single and unambiguous blueprint for a Christian ordering of society actually exists; the freedom to serve one's neighbor includes the possibility that the common welfare may indeed be the kind of destination for which quite diverse route plans may seem feasible. Thus the very program that appeals to some consciences may repel others; whether in fact each is an exemplar of love must be the subject of difficult and searching analysis. Finally a further difficulty arises from the circumstance that specific programs may only partially realize the vision of the gospel; the ambiguities of "integration" as it has occurred in many American communities should warn us not to assume easy answers.

All of these considerations taken together remind us that the *simul,* the inescapable dialectical tension, is present at every level and in every decision. Dealing with problems as complex as those of the sixties, Christian moralists needed to be highly sensitive to the varieties of interests, options, and agendas available. But in the format of modern religious gatherings, where the delegates often find themselves hurried and harried, where the leadership cannot overlook the public impact of what is said, policy-makers find themselves driven to recommendations that are both brief and clear, circumstances under which the kinds of qualifications theologians are prone to make tend to get lost. Especially in the turmoil that would not subside, when action seemed urgent, religious decision-makers tended to oversimplify issues, to stress the righteous qualities of recommended programs rather than their limited nature. The pressures operated to define the issues in terms of "we" and "they," the good side and the evil one. Political differences hardened into battle lines.

Conservative church people may have even greater difficulties with social action pronouncements. What precisely is the status of a statement on social justice which has been given an apparently clear biblical warrant? Surely the authority of the Word belongs to any such pronouncement? We have difficulty understanding that the pronouncements of ecclesiastical assemblies — not just on issues of social justice — are human judgments, partial approximations, not absolutes, no matter how necessary or how correct they eventually turn out to be. Conservatives may well have difficulty accepting these limitations. Convinced that the task of ecclesiastical assemblies is to bear witness to divine truth, convinced as well that their own theological convictions founded on scriptural warrants possess this character of truth, they would seem to be driven to the position that any social pronouncements which in their understanding clearly derive from the Scriptures or scripturally sound doctrine, must also be as fully authoritative as the original premises. The position of Roman Catholic conservatives on abortion, of Protestants on the use of alcoholic beverages, illustrates how moral reasoning of this kind operates.

Complex social issues, especially when change in deeply embedded habits or organizational practices is called for, frequently bring about situations in which both sides may claim their positions as the only correct application of Scripture and doctrine. The result can easily be unseemly controversy and schism. It is easier to avoid the issues. In both the liberal and the conservative situation the ideology of consensus contributes to the difficulty of decision-making.

The ideology of consensus operated not only within the various religious groups but also among the cadres of ecclesiastical leaders in the main line denominations. Not only as advocates of social action but as participants in and protagonists of ecumenical cooperation, these leaders differed from many of their fellow ministers as well as from the laity. Their common ideology, along with the networks of acquaintance among many of them, has provided their critics with an "Eastern religious establishment" at which they could aim their polemical shafts. Sociologically, as well as theologically, the rank and file might well feel that they are neither listened to nor ministered to. The styles of thought of the professional elite, more in tune with contemporary theological trends and with the latest developments on the ecumenical scene, could not help but appear foreign to those who found themselves working with older traditions. Under these circumstances irrelevant but deep-seated considerations might contribute to hostility towards social action proposals.

Theological methodology further complicates the ideological problem. Any perusal of most denominational statements will soon reveal a rather typical format — an elaborate theological discussion must provide the basis for the ethical posture. We must somehow assume that a Christian witness springs from Christian premises. Evidently, it will not do to respond spontaneously to injustice, or to react simply on grounds of human decency. We have to bring the problem into the realm of theological discourse. Ideologically we have to put our own stamp on it — a Lutheran position on race, a Presbyterian paper on population, a Methodist witness on abortion. And so on. (I have exaggerated somewhat, but the pattern is all too prevalent.)

Organizational Imperialism

The organizational imperialism of the religious groups effectively prevented either the resources of the organizations or the energies of their members from being directed to new undertakings on any adequate scale. More important, perhaps, organizational imperialism obscured the view of many Christians for new possibilities.

Social welfare offers the paradigmatic instance; we have vast programs of religious social welfare: Catholic Welfare, Lutheran Social Service, Presbyterian health agencies, Methodist hospitals, and so on. A great deal of energy and time has been spent over the years both in the operation of these separate enterprises and in developing denominational justifications for involvement. Along with these commitments to denominational enterprises have come the natural alliances with private social agencies and the social work professionals, who have a great investment in the voluntary agency establishment. Thus the welfare professionals of the main line denominations have in fact devoted relatively little time or attention until very recently to the great and pressing issues of public welfare. Consequently the major religious groups have made relatively little effort to get their members concerned to take a long hard look at how public welfare is operating. Although by and large the church professionals have supported welfare reform, and at national gatherings appropriate resolutions have been passed, one can hardly say that the public sector ever became a serious subject of study in the local religious groups — the very people who could have discovered much about the inhumanity of public welfare without ever leaving their home territories.

Religiously sponsored welfare programs played a crucial role in the development of the social services in the United States. Originally many of them were interdenominational efforts (although Congregationalists and Presbyterians probably played the largest role.) Many of the great private social agencies and organizations grew out of the cooperative efforts of the evangelical pioneers. They also gradually grew away from explicit religious identification. More recently, as social welfare received a more recognized place in the activities of religious groups, agencies and programs developed which were explicitly under the sponsorship and control of the denominations. Thus the Protestant social welfare empire developed.

Both the private agencies and the church-related ones for the most part treated public welfare as a second-rate affair. The individualistic ethic dominating most Protestants made this relatively easy. The generally backward condition of public welfare, itself the obverse of its neglect, simply seemed to strengthen the prejudices against it. While in the upper echelons much has changed, the old attitudes still persist. The chief victims here, of course, are the poor.

None of this suggests that we should not have private agencies. But it does suggest that the religious groups need to re-examine their relationships to their own agencies, declare many of them "of age" and let them fend for themselves. This step might free the denominations and their welfare professionals to give more adequate attention to the larger issues.

The major evangelical enterprises founded in the early part of the last century were not denominational enterprises; the American Tract Society, the American Bible Society, the American Sunday School Union, although denominational groups affiliated themselves with these organizations. The YMCA and YWCA are late nineteenth century examples. Denominational approval generally meant that funds could be solicited in the congregations of the denomination. The associations explicitly committed to social reform, particularly the abolitionist societies, although clearly the result of an evangelical impetus, were not church-related. They were private voluntary associations. They drew large degrees of support from some religious circles; most of their members were probably active church people. But jurisdictionally they were independent.

But we have learned little from this pattern. During the crisis of the 1960s, many of the denominations began to develop urban crisis programs that reflected the continuation of the imperialistic mentality. The monies and the leadership efforts that went into these programs, had they been put into the hands of groups like the National Urban League, the NAACP, the Southern Christian Leadership Conference, and so on, without strings attached, might have made a critical difference in many situations. Even in the crisis situation most religious groups could not let go of their controls. Only programs they approved had a chance of funding.

Despite the limited nature of the response which the religious groups made because of the inherent ideology of imperialism, each new step often generated heated debate and resistance. Actually over against the inherited budgetary commitments to the institutions of the past, the new programs were financially undernourished and politically they had little structural security in the ecclesiastical bureaucracies.

Existing structures for effective social action through the churches have fundamental flaws: the ideology of consensus can, on the one hand, blunt clearcut action in order not to offend a resisting or apathetic segment of the membership, especially when that group constitutes a numerical but inarticulate majority; the same ideology can, on the other hand, through the operating structures of ecclesiastical hierarchies and religious assemblies present a "united front" of commitment, for which the membership feels no ownership, in which it does not participate. Organizational imperialism, at the same time, tends to channel such action as occurs on large-scale social problems into relatively narrow channels of church-controlled programming. Only in rare moments of a widespread sense of injustice can the religious groups really act effectively. A better strategy is needed.

5

A PLEA FOR PARTISANSHIP

It is my fundamental thesis that if church members are serious about social change, about racism and war, poverty and blight, *the place for them to be active is in secular organizations committed to social change, in organizations independent of ecclesiastical control, budgetary and structural.* Above all, if these Christians want to be effective, political organizations are the best available vehicles.

"Political" organizations include more than partisan groups, i.e., Republican, Democratic, and other parties seeking support at the polls. All organizations are political that aim at changing or protecting social structures in the public arena, whether by legislation or lobbying, by direct or indirect access to those who make decisions that affect the larger organization of public life. Thus the American Medical Association clearly engages in political activity, just as does the AFL-CIO, and the League of Women Voters. The National Urban League working through corporate hierarchies, especially in seeking equal opportunities in employment, is in these respects a "political" organization.

One of the characteristic features of the American scene has been the abundance of organizations available to mobilize persons in behalf of some cause. "Voluntary association" independent of any direct tie to a religious group was the vehicle which the early abolitionists used. Their rhetoric was clearly religious, as indeed their primary motives were, and they made effective use of the methods they had learned in the frontier revivals, but organizationally they remained separate from the religious denominations of their day. Similarly, "voluntary associations," functioning as intermediary organizations, as a number of researches have pointed out, have helped build political power for ethnic minorities in the past. The outcome of recent work in community organization, not the least the work which IFCO has been supporting, is beginning to achieve similar results for black, Chicano, and Indian groups. Over and above these particular situations in which voluntary associations have functioned in political processes, we must recognize that in all American communities large numbers of these organizations exist and play important roles in community decision-making. Voluntary association provides Christian citizens with an appropriate tool for affecting the political process and achieving social change.

"Christians are members of more than one socially defined community," as James Gustafson has pointed out. "We are," he continues, "engaged in social action as Christians in the various communities to which we belong." One significant opportunity for Christians thus can be and ought to be the witness they can bring through the organizations to which they belong. To follow Gustafson's argument a step further, Christians can through joining together with other like-minded people develop significant political blocs on a particular issue. In effect the Commission on Race and Religion did just this on the filibuster issue in 1964.

To do something of this kind regularly, however, Christians must accept the legitimacy of action through the existing political organizations or through the creation of new ones. *Religious leadership ought to encourage action in the secular arena,* not to press for the development of church-related programs. Commitment to social change means choosing up sides; it means dealing with questions of power, with established structures, with the need for new legislation. This is what political involvement is all about, whether through explicitly partisan organizations or through non-partisan ones. Effective religious action for social justice requires commitment both to causes and to the existing political parties or to new ones. Meaningful commitment will require partisanship. Partisanship can best be pursued outside the official religious groups.

Encouraging their memberships to join "secular" organizations will not free the religious groups from internal controversy over social issues. Nor is that the intent of these recommendations. The recommendations seek rather to direct efforts for social change into channels where Christians of many denominational persuasions but with a common ethical commitment and non-Christians who share the commitments can join together for more effective action.

A second recommendation logically belongs here. I believe denominations (and local congregations as well) should make financial contributions to these organizations rather than attempt to establish programs and recruit staff on their own. They should also encourage their members individually to contribute to these organizations. Social justice questions are not normally denominational issues, for which "our church" should seek credit; they are community-wide and national questions. We should deal with them on this basis. In the field of community organizations, as already noted, IFCO represents an effort of this kind.

I recognize that an early result of the adoption of the policy here recommended may be that budgets and direct benevolence giving (especially to the mainline churches) will decline. Individual Christians will be free to use their benevolence giving for causes to which they have strong emotional commitments. This does not disturb me in the least; I have long believed that the best measure of Christian benevolence is what gets done in the community in seeing that human needs are met and not what appears in denominational stewardship reports.

American Christians are already involved in party politics,

The results of survey research have provided ample documentation of this involvement. But the commitments are often implicit, ideological, more a matter of communal tradition than of ethical awareness; uncomfortable questions about the relationship between what we believe and what we do as party members are often avoided. We ought to make these questions explicit and unavoidable.

Interestingly enough, the McGovern crusade in the Democratic party provided an instance of such explicit commitment on the part of many persons, although more often from secular than from religious convictions. Prohibition was clearly an earlier, more explicit involvement, including the formation of a third party. The original organization of the Republican party included elements of explicit religious commitment. My quarrel as a politician with the McGovern crusade centers more on its political ineptitude after Miami than in the causes it espoused. By and large, its radicalism on most questions was overstated; but one cannot fault the moral seriousness of many of its most committed adherents. Unfortunately, they acted more like foolish virgins than like innocent doves; after Miami they evidently lost whatever cunning they had ever possessed.

Political commitment through partisan organizations need not be the only kind of organized effort in which individual Christians participate. Indeed it cannot be, for our communities abound in organized efforts dealing with questions of moral concern. Informed participation includes being aware of the political commitments, generally implicit, of "nonpolitical" groups.

Any organizatiton working at tasks designed to serve the welfare of others has already made a political commitment. The commitment is not necessarily partisan, although in most struggles partisan involvements will become an issue. Most of the objections to the involvement of religious groups in political action comes from people on the other side. This is only natural.

Not all groups working to promote the public welfare are

without selfish interests. In fact many of the groups most effective in the public arena have as their avowed goal serving the interests of their memberships. For the most part they also claim that the interests of their membership and the public interest overlap, if they are not identical. Chambers of Commerce, labor organizations, the American Medical Association and similar groups are clearly serving their memberships.

The rhetoric of American politics requires that the public utterances of these groups claim that their primary concern is for the common good. In most instances this is not hypocritical; its advocates probably assume that what furthers their interests also furthers the common good. Such claims have a partial truth. But it is a partial truth that needs critical scrutiny; implicit commitments need to be made explicit. Consequences of policies must be tracked down.

A probable outcome should be public debate, loud and sometimes noisy, emotionally colored quarreling. Nothing could be healthier but too often the ideology of consensus, the public rhetoric of serving the general welfare, precludes debate. Most organizations do not tolerate internal dissent; factionalism is abhorred. Nor do most organizations enjoy public debates with other organizations; quarreling is unseemly. Public discussion of issues takes place on a very limited basis.

Even good government groups, e.g., the League of Women Voters, are not exempt from the effects of the ideology of consensus. Considering some of the touchy issues local chapters have studied, the absence of prolonged debate can only be viewed as surprising. Surely not all of the problems have a single obvious solution. More probably, although officially non-partisan, the League may well reflect the political understandings of the kinds of persons that make up the bulk of its memberships, the well to do and established rather than the little people. Non-partisan movements of this kind rarely come up with radical or controversial answers.

What turns devout Christians off is probably not only the

abhorrence of public quarreling, but also their religious aversion to pursuing "self-interest." Many Christians feel that the pursuit of self-interest in politics is in itself morally wrong. A literal application of Luther's distinction between "for self, for others" would apparently support only a politics of unselfishness. But the problem does not solve itself this easily. Luther's principle of the *simul* suggests that we view with considerable suspicion those who claim their politics is pure. We are probably deceiving ourselves even when we deal only with individual persons and their ideals.

When we deal with group activity, as Reinhold Niebuhr reminded us decades ago, we must call into question the claim to have a program of "pure and unselfish ideals." Even when the goals are praiseworthy, organized groups quickly become enamored both of power and of their own recognition and survival. The crusader for sacred causes, as history should teach us, often becomes shrilly self-righteous. He quickly succumbs to the temptation that the rightness of his cause permits him to use means that he would forbid others to use. The Prohibition crusade remains as the great American experiment in the corruption of the righteous. The recent troubles of the Nixon White House Staff may be a second example.

Paradoxically the *simul* suggests that realism about human shortcomings may make it probable that the road to the public welfare leads through the encounter of interest groups with one another. Nothing as ideal as Milton's marketplace of ideas is here presupposed. The forum may itself be under the control of hostile forces; the debate may be something other than the clash of ideas arranged in logical arguments. The point simply is that we shall not secure justice by attempting to work only through saintly people and incorruptible organizations of impeccable probity; it is "in, with, and under" the worldly struggle of different interest groups that justice must be served.

For the dictatorship of the partisans of a single sacred cause, whether avowedly Christian or avowedly un-Christian, has more often served the oppressors and the persecutors, served the causes of conformity, censorship, and concentration camps. The free flow of factionalism and the multiplication of factions in an open society provides the best guarantee of the pursuit of welfare.

These are arguments of No. 10 of *The Federalist Papers*. Like all political arguments they must be carefully scrutinized. They were written to secure votes for the United States Constitution. They were designed to prove that the Constitution served the cause of liberty.

Despite the obvious partisanship, Madison's argument in this paper is fundamentally sound. The price of "order," in which criticism is muted, opposition is discouraged, includes not only freedom but also justice. There is no such animal as a neutral ruling class, an impartial chief executive, an infallible leader. Factionalism, debate, disorder—no matter how much they may trouble the efficiency experts among certain organizational theorists—are essential qualities of a free society. It is better to make one's interests explicit than to pretend to have none.

Programs and performance cannot be assumed to be identical. Every political administration needs critics to point out its shortcomings; every successfully executed program represents the success of some group or groups in gaining attention to its interests. At the same same time some groups have been left out. The history of American politics from generation to generation records the struggle of groups trying to get it. The struggle continues for blacks, for Chicanos, for Indians, for women. The struggle will continue. The struggle of pressure groups with one another is not a guarantee of justice; it does represent opportunity.

In these struggles the formal political parties have a major part. Political parties are not gatherings of saints. In this respect they are no different from other groups. What makes the political party different is its direct linkage with governmental processes. When a party has gained power, its members not only occupy the major executive, legislative, and judicial offices, but they are in the position to enact their programs into law and to execute their policies. While such consequences are never automatic, since campaign promises are not always fulfilled and are sometimes not fulfillable, nevertheless parties are major instruments through which the common good of the community can be served.

Precisely because parties play this role we find powerful interests working within them and seeking to affect their platforms and performances. Thus both within parties and between them we may find considerable differences of opinion; clashes of interest frequently occur. The stake of various groups in the outcome gradually becomes evident. Under optimum conditions every hand is eventually called; all the cards must be played face up on the table. While these conditions rarely prevail, while some groups prefer not to have their interests uncovered, while some politicians are the willing captives of special interests, the role of the opposition in a healthy political climate is always to push for greater publicity, greater openness. (This is also the role of the press; Watergate is an important chapter in its history.) Effective opposition is an institutionalized expression of the *simul*.

The conception of the political party advocated here is explicitly non-ideological in the European sense. This does not deny major differences between two primary American political parties, Republicans and Democrats. The two political parties represent different constituencies, have different political styles, yet both tend to be pragmatic in program construction. From the European point of view the American variety of politics is strikingly unideological. From the Christion point of view this kind of politics offers opportunity for participation in a struggle free of some of the ideological and moral traps not unknown in public life. Effective participation and partisanship go hand in hand.

A Christian political party is a misnomer. Such an organization not only claims too much, identifying loyalty to Jesus Christ with particular programs, but it also involves an inherent judgment of self-righteousness. It defines the struggle in the wrong terms. (It is unfortunately true that in some

European countries the political process has in part polarized in these terms; generally an abuse of religious establishment is in part involved.)

Positive reasons also exist for participating in groups serving a multitude of interests. The broad range of human needs rarely can be encompassed within the platform of a group serving a single interest or subservient to a particular ideology. In specific situations of injustice, of course, a narrow range of agitation and organization may be strategically and morally preferable. But quite frequently two of the great concerns of the democratic revolution of the last several centuries, freedom and equality, tend to work at cross-purposes. (Fraternity is probably more an outcome than a program.) Within a coalition of interests the dialectic of freedom and equality can play itself out with rough justice; without equality the premises of freedom become illusory for many people; without freedom equality may approximate slavery rather than humanity. The political parties as coalitions of interests may be the best available—by no means perfect—instruments for getting both freedom and equality.

A coalition of interests assumes, although it does not guarantee, built-in correctives of self-criticism within each political party. For the *simul* requires constant self-examination as a condition of health. Party leadership quite often resists the questions of dissatisfied groups. But it resists their questions and their correctives at the risk of losing voters, of losing elections, of failing to gain or hold public office. Thus the principle of self-criticism does work although by no means adequately. Indeed Christians in public life, aware of the need for self-examination, could play a needed role in maintaining openness in parties.

Where parties fail, other options are open. The independent voter—if he is genuinely independent, not just too lazy, too indifferent, or too afraid to wear a party label—provides one corrective. A goodly number of voters, even those with party affiliations, are swing voters. Normally Republican farmers in the Midwest go Democratic when farm prices fall, normally

partisan voters of either party may be sufficiently disenchanted with a particular office-holder (often for good reasons)
to cross party lines for a particular office.

Independent voting is clearly a Christian option. It is normally more effective as a veto or as a vote of confidence than
as a positive political act. Sometimes—when the power of office has been severely abused—the veto is essential. It is another way the *simul* expresses itself. At other times the vote
of confidence is of critical importance. To return a political
leader to office who has increased taxes, or who has moved
into unfamiliar territory, is an important judgment. In 1936
and 1940 American voters, despite the fears of the privileged,
voted their confidence in Franklin D. Roosevelt. In a crucial
referendum in Ohio in 1972 the voters sustained the State
income tax which Democratic Governor John Gilligan had
courageously won from a hostile legislature.

6

THE AGENDA OF
MIDDLE AMERICANS

Third Parties and Middle Americans

Third parties in American politics have rarely been successful at the polls; they have almost always signaled major moral and political crises in American public life. The Progressive movement of 1912 marked the beginning of the exodus of the WASP intellectuals from the Republican party. 1932 and thereafter saw many of them in the Franklin Roosevelt camp, some in his cabinet.

The third party movements and the civil rights and foreign policy crises of the period since World War II are a little more difficult to analyze. The protest movement which George Wallace has headed is at this point more significant than the Thurmond Dixiecrats or the right wing ideologues leading the American Independent party. The significance of the Dixiecrats has been—much to the chagrin of many Northern Republicans—to bring into Republican ranks the most reactionary and racist elements in Southern politics. The quid pro quo has evidently been support of the economic interests which have had so strong a voice in Northern Republican councils. Thus on both the question of race and of economic justice the Republican party has taken on a more elitist character.

The argument just presented must be weighed for what it says and for what it does not say. Both political parties have racist elements; both have elitist elements; both have advocates of special economic privilege in their midst (we need only note the influence of oil and mining interests in the Democratic party.)

Racism is a vicious sin; it is a major destructive force in American political life. But the case for racial eqality is preeminently a moral case; the scientific data, no matter how important, are secondary; what comes first is the equal moral worth of every human being. But moral causes are not demonstrable in the laboratory. The disagreements must be settled in the public arena, as well as in the consciences of Christians. We can demand of the Strom Thurmonds and their kind that they be honest about their attitudes—as they can demand of us. We can also hope that they will vanish as a long obsolescent species. But we cannot simply brush their existence aside or ignore their political base. We must deal with them in the public arena; this is where they must be defeated and repudiated.

The rise of George Wallace to national prominence as a political leader is a more complex phenomenon than an analysis in terms of racism alone can describe. The populist appeal of the Alabama governor to certain segments of the Northern working class and white ethnic vote needs to be seen as more than white backlash, an easy liberal response; we must not forget that in different ways Robert Kennedy also tapped these blocs of votes.

Two components converge in the rise of the Wallace movement: first, the failure of white political leadership, while it had the chance to carry through on the promise of the civil rights movement. The tragedy of white political leadership in the civil rights movement, even before 1954 and particularly after that date, lies first of all in the failure of their moral commitment to full equality. As a consequence of the moral failure, there followed the failure to devote adequate resources to secure effective administration, to carry through full-fledged programs of education to bring the citizens most affected, both white and black, to a fuller understanding that justice and American values demanded a genuinely equal society.

By default—and by intent as well—black groups were left to carry the burden of the change, especially in the most difficult situations. Often, indeed, generally, they lacked adequate resources. The white liberals, including the churches, who could and did provide some of the wherewithall, did not themselves fully understand nor easily accept all the consequences of equal black participation. Meanwhile ample resources were available to the opposition. Lack of commitment at the highest levels in Washington encouraged resistance. The apparent need under the conditions that developed to resort to coercion backed up with police power bred resentment among the black populations of many urban centers. Blacks felt frustration, anger, alienation. Even in the earliest expressions of black power white liberals were uncomfortable; more radical expressions were given a visibility that not only spotlighted failure, but that also listed demands that began to arouse the distrust, eventually the opposition, of many working class whites.

The second component then is the rising anger of middle Americans. Nothing said here should be interpreted to suggest that working class and ethnic whites had a shining record on questions of racial justice. Serious problems exist in many sectors of this middle stratum of citizens. But the fact remains that these persons, particularly in many major urban concentrations, provided the voting majorities for liberal members of Congress who served as sponsors for civil rights and other reform legislation. At the same time their own prosperity and success has been greatly exaggerated. Often only with the help of a moon-lighting job, or a fully employed wife, did many of these persons reach the level of income that might be considered affluent. Many of them resided in neighborhoods of cities in which the schools, the housing, and the public services were just as inadequate as those in the ghetto.

Furthermore they were in fact the major victims of the operations of an unjust tax structure, a burden that became increasingly heavy in a continuing inflationary economy. They in
fact had good grounds for feeling that they were the neglected
Americans, pushed around, asked to pay the cost, serving their
country on the battlefields of Vietnam; they became increasingly angry Americans.

The moral single-mindedness of some of the leaders of the
protest movements, no matter how commendable as a matter
of principle, often foundered on the rocks of misguided
strategy. Too often the concern for "making a witness" obscured the necessary strategic question: will this particular
protest in fact win more adherents to our cause? Rightly or
wrongly, many middle Americans saw more wilfullness than
idealism in some forms of demonstration. Knowing their own
limited economic circumstances, many white working people
saw black demands as a threat to themselves rather than as
a step in the direction of greater justice. In the peace movement and in the counter-culture they saw values which they
held dear openly flouted. In many instances indeed the style
of the protests triggered resistance and anger, and the merits
of an issue never became the subject of attention. Meanwhile
what they felt were their own legitimate grievances were dismissed. American workers were now, according to many authorities, living in an affluent society, prosperous and secure.
Thus each side saw the other through the distorted grid of
convenient stereotypes; working with a misdirected definition
of the situation, both contributed to one another's frustration
and anger.

We will not solve the questions of racial justice, which are
matters of top priority, without dealing with the problems of
economic justice. Without a concern for the welfare of all
citizens, without a fuller understanding of what it means to
be committed to the welfare of the neighbor, we cannot deal
with the anger of middle Americans nor the anger of black
Americans, Chicanos, and Indians. Nor without this fuller
vision will we deal with the problems of sexual discrimination

and equitable participation on the part of all generations of Americans in the full benefits of our society. Economic measures alone will not usher in an equalitarian society, but without economic reform the major problems cannot be solved. To pour more money into the apparently bottomless pit of bad programs is stupid, politically and morally as well as economically. But money will also be needed to finance more effective alternatives.

Our first step must therefore be to demythologize the widespread belief in the affluence of the American worker. In 1966, for example, when the figures reached their highest point in years, less than three out of every five persons in the labor force worked full time for 50-52 weeks a year. Two out of every five persons worked less; many were in fact only "peripheral workers" and had been such for many years. While women, the young, the old, and the blacks contributed disproportionately to the number of peripheral workers, nevertheless large numbers of other workers, even in the highly organized building trades and the steel and auto unions, did not work full time all year long. Large numbers of Americans did not earn even a minimum decent level of living, sometimes even with more than one member of the household in the labor force. Many of these peripheral workers also had the lowest fringe benefits in terms of medical care, unemployment compensation, eventual social security benefits. Since 1966 inflation has put even greater pressure on the pocketbooks of middle Americans, white collar as well as blue collar.

Even if middle Americans are wrong in the objects of their anger, they nevertheless resent being pushed around. If for no other reason than his own poverty and powerlessness, the economically pressed white person, equally the victim of economic exploitation, feels highly resentful. Because liberal politicians—defining the reaction of many working people simply as "white backlash"—tended to ignore and at times to castigate these voters, their claims to be advocates of full social justice lost credibility. Furthermore, the manifest fact that many "reform" programs worked more to the benefit of the well to do, to the enrichment of certain vested interests, while the problems themselves grew worse, for black and white alike—medical care, urban renewal, public welfare—fed a growing distrust of the liberal leadership. We should not wonder that social protest swelled into the electoral victories of George Wallace.

Thus the third party movement of the 1970s must be seen not merely as racist, but as also in many ways the revolt of frustrated citizens. At the same time this revolt must be seen as a serious danger signal. George Wallace is not Hitler; facile parallels are too easy. But the American political situation has characteristics in common with the political situation in Weimar Germany. Unless certain problems are given more constructive solutions, the polarization of American society could continue. As the recent investigation surrounding the Watergate case and the Ellsberg trial make clear, the Nixon administration suffered from the consequences of a political paranoia. Under the pretext (probably held with some sincerity) of national security, former President Nixon's inner circle introduced elements of political surveillance, the use of provocateurs, and the suppression of dissent into American political life on a scale that politicized government agencies at the Washington level into a threat to constitutional freedom. The failure to deal with protest and dissent openly, the resort to the tactics of polarization, reflects a mentality that is fundamentally out of touch with political freedom. It is a mentality that as history shows can use scapegoating effectively for its own ends.

We cannot ignore as misguided the deep distrust of the political process which many Americans have and which Watergate has done so much to strengthen and confirm. Even apart from this highly publicized event too much evidence exists that certain lobbying groups are highly effective not only in Congress but in sabotaging the very regulatory agencies established to watch over certain industries. The situation in some state legislatures is even more scandalous. Structural reforms are needed. Public business should be done as publicly as possible.

At the same time we must recognize that deep-seated cleavages do exist on certain issues. Our responses to these issues will often be highly charged emotionally. On the other hand, despite certain cleavages, we must also recognize that critics from both the right and the left have agreed on certain problems, though not necessarily on their solutions. Thus we hear from both the left and the right that American foreign policy has too long been the monopoly of a small leadership elite from both parties who share a common outlook best reflected in the extent to which the membership of the Council on Foreign Relations overlaps with the possession of key policy-making places in the State Department. The lack of responsiveness of many governmental agencies to the needs of the little people, while quick to answer the complaints of the well-heeled vested interests, contributes to the feeling of disillusionment many Americans (the young and the black, as well as white middle Americans) have about the political process and the two major political parties. Under these circumstances third parties serve as moral and political critics of the major parties. They provide a criticism these parties ought to be making themselves.

Power must always be criticized. Power must never be allowed to become absolute. The very existence of two parties, especially since each has some structural basis in office-holding, relativizes power. The party system is thus a kind of institutionalization of human limitations; when this structure apparently fails, third parties move into the scene. Thus the *simul* finds structural recognition.

An effective opposition party is always the watchdog for the abuse of power. The exposing of public sinners is one of its vital functions. Negative as such criticism often appears, self-righteous though its language may be when it is obviously serving a partisan interest, we can understand it theologically. It is the political equivalent of preaching the law; it is Nathan pointing the finger of accusation and announcing, "You are the man."

More can be said. For effective opposition to power, especially to the exercise of power and its abuse, must be moral criticism. The voter generally gives short shrift to the candidate whose only program is to get his snout into the trough in place of his opponent's. Power to be effectively criticized must be considered in moral terms.

Power and Justice

Morality here means political morality, social justice, not just personal probity. We Americans still have a great deal to learn about criticism of this kind. Our churches and our schools, as well as our politicians, our newspapers, and so on, have served us poorly, because we are more adept at throwing out the scoundrels than at expelling the oppressors.

The Christian concern for social justice is therefore vitally necessary. We owe much to the pragmatism and realism of Reinhold Niebuhr, particularly to his *Moral Man and Immoral Society,* which taught many of us that the canons of personal ethics were inadequate for the analysis of structural problems. But certain Christian realists, wanting to be more orthodox than their master, have made power so great a factor that morality and justice have become secondary concerns. Power needs moral analysis, an analysis appropriate to its structures and its possibilities. Political realism slowed down the Kennedy initiative in civil rights; too many of the intelligentsia concurred. Political realism led many of the same intelligentsia into support for the Vietnam war, indeed support for the escalation of 1965. *The Pentagon Papers* carry many of the names; they carry a sorry documentation of how power can seduce highly trained minds into political immorality. Power always needs moral criticism.

Moral criticism should be the particular role of the "outs." It should also be the role of the religious teachers—and of the ordinary Christian—through the church and through other media, including the political party. Power can corrupt any-one—only constant critical scrutiny can hold power in check.

Other countries, especially our enemies, can also play this role. We ought therefore to listen to them carefully. We need not agree with them, but at the very least we must hear what they are saying. We will see ourselves in the mirror of their opinions. The picture may be an ugly one; before we reject it, we should discover why they see us as they do. It is too easy to take umbrage at the criticisms of others; it is not always easy to learn from them. At the very least we should lose our illusions.

What has been said about the criticism of power also applies to the critique of programs. No party platform will bring in the kingdom of God; nor will any party usher in a human utopia. Very few proposals do much more than advance tentative solutions of varying plausibility. All of them need moral scrutiny in terms of the criteria of social justice.

Political programs are important. Indeed no candidate and no party should be taken seriously if no program is offered. Christians who would rely only on spontaneity, goodness, and religiosity are simply naive. We have a right to know the direction in which leaders want to move. We cannot deal with problems without directions.

Information, the best possible information from a variety of sources is also necessary to evaluate programs. As Christians we need to do our homework. Reason and experience are the tools we have in common with our fellow citizens. With them, with our command of the data and the persuasiveness of our concern for the personhood of the other, the opponent, as well as our commitment to compassion and social justice, we must make our case.

Since programs are not absolutes, other options can never be ruled out a priori. Nor can compromise be ruled out. Compromise can be a step in the right direction. Or it can be a defeat. The relativity of programs does not mean that any-thing goes, that victory is unimportant, or that it is impossible to determine better or worse alternatives. Only the dogmatic really can avoid the hard work of thinking or the careful examination of experience. Christian consciousness of the limited nature of every program cannot afford the luxury of doing nothing.

Programs no matter how good must be seen in terms of what they actually do to people. Administration is as important as legislation. Bureaucratic bungling or indifference, the dominance of routine, can dehumanize the best of programs. Every organization becomes interested in having a smooth operation, in keeping harmony in the office—sometimes the client pays. He serves the organization; the organization no longer serves him.

Opposition parties are sometimes effective critics of bad administration. So are pressure groups and dissatisfied clients. But governing parties, even in their own self-interest, should also be critical. The political party, particularly the local organization at county and precinct levels, can often be both the listening post for the frustrated and the ombudsman for the confused. Thus the party leadership can intervene creatively where bureaucratic routine has smothered personhood.

Finally programs can be criticized for lack of direction, for lack of vision. The Christian vision of social justice in a free and equal society can be brought into play at this point. Vision may indeed be one of the major Christian contributions to the political process.

A democratic party system should and can express both the limitations and the possibilities in human government. As such the party system gives embodiment to the *simul*; it can also express the dialectic between collegiality and hierarchy.

Not all Christians see the political process from the same perspective. We need not go into the reasons for the differences which may be many, a goodly number quite possibly non-theological in nature.

Collegiality and hierarchy express two basic differences in political style: populism and elitism. These differences can be seen both as differences of political commitment and as related facets of political structure. Hierarchy addresses the problem of authority, the need for a decision-making locus, and the need for a population that generally obeys the existing laws. Hierarchy involves more than having generals to give orders or presidents to issue directives. It means lawmakers willing to vote as conscience dictates, as more than simply the mirror image of the majority prejudices of their supporters. Hierarchy means judges faithful in discharge of their duties even against the grain of their own political preferences. Hierarchy calls for responsible exercise of authority.

Responsibility does not exist in a vacuum. The fracturing of power in the American system of checks and balances sometimes makes it difficult to determine who is responsible for particular programs. Responsibility within a representative democracy means responsibility to the people, the voters. Hierarchy can be kept responsible only where collegiality functions effectively.

Collegiality does not mean that the majority can do as it pleases. The voice of the people is not the voice of God— except relatively, tentatively, under critical scrutiny. Collegiality does not exist where disenfranchisement has occurred— *de facto* or *de jure*. Full collegiality is still a goal, not a fact.

Full collegiality also means a free and responsible voter. In any given election we must on the one hand take the voter as he is; we must also seek to make him better. Actions and programs that undermine responsibility must be called into question. Hierarchy must thus in the final analysis be subordinated to collegiality; in a properly collegial society hierarchy is always a matter of delegation, not of possession; it always includes accountability.

The Christian's role in this process is a double one. He will have his preferences. He will also recognize a further responsibility, namely, that from his perspective the entire process— in, with, and under the human decisions—works within the framework of God's intentions. The Christian must therefore not only apply the *simul*, recognizing the fallibility, the shortcomings of every program, every authority, every franchise, every election, but he must also seek out the particular opportunities for witness to the purposes of God. This he will do humbly, for he is not God. But this he must do, because he must witness.

Our generation has been called upon to make a particular witness about war; it may also be called upon to make a particular witness about human equality and about the care of the earth. If these statements are true, the Christian will not only seek to have these questions high on the political agenda, but he will also encourage discussion within the political community. Thus he will also speak to the conscience of his time through these channels, as well as through his political work. For he is not just a partisan; he is always and first of all a Christian, putting loyalty to Jesus Christ first.

7

LOVE PLUS SOCIAL ACTION

For quite some years now a major moral issue confronting the voters of a number of states has been whether or not to legalize a state lottery.

There is a good *prima facie* case against lotteries. Lotteries are a very bad way to finance public services, not because they involve a "sin" called gambling (which flourishes in our country whether it is inside or outside the law), but because there is no relationship between ability to pay and the amounts an individual wagers. In short, a public lottery is another tax for which the poor may bear the chief burden.

But I am not going to mount a campaign against the lottery. Not because I do not care, but because quite simply I can list a dozen items that deserve a higher moral priority than this one.

There is also a theological and sociological case that can be made. I shall come to it in a moment. The recent referendum on a lottery in Ohio revealed something very interesting about the relationship between religion and politics that needs prior attention.

Almost without exception on the issue of state lotteries the church people of Ohio and other states have managed to mount substantial campaigns. Church publications carry the announcements; literature is made available; sermons are delivered from many Protestant pulpits. The *Ohio Christian News,* the house organ of the Ohio Council of Churches, carried extended materials on the lottery campaign.

To the best of my knowledge, very few parishioners protested that their ministers were mixing religion and politics. They didn't dare—"gambling" is a moral issue.

Evidently institutionalized racism, the welfare mess, the neglect of the poor, the maldistribution of health care services, the inhumanity of elements of our correctional system—to mention a few major political issues of our day—are not "moral" issues. On most of them the churches have never organized a political campaign. The few that some hardy souls have brought before officials have generated controversies, led to backlash and polarization.

This is not to say that there have not been ecclesiastical resolutions on these questions. We have had bushel baskets full. We have had excellent studies as well. But we have not had officially, ecclesiastically initiated campaigns, in which church publications and church leaders could without fear of contradiction set down the moral line for the faithful to follow. We have not had campaign treasuries, large-scale lobbying, ecumenical cooperation involving even the most conservative of the religious groups. Only in the Civil Rights campaign of 1964 was there equivalent ecclesiastical leadership and organization; even then, the scale of cooperation was not nearly as broad as can be found in any anti-lottery crusade. The campaign against the Vietnam war was not, for the most part, ever a campaign in which the denominations officially provided leadership and organization. Special action groups, as well as the traditional peace-oriented groups, such as the Fellowship of Reconciliation, carried the brunt of that campaign.

Like other state councils of churches, the Ohio Council does a certain amount of legislative lobbying with somewhat mixed results. The lobbying attempts to implement positions which the representatives of the member churches have supported in the General Assembly of the council. Such activity is perfectly proper; by and large, however, most of the clergy and laity in the member organizations pay little attention to this particular activity. On most issues many other groups will be engaged in lobbying; unless an issue catches public attention, however, the press pays little attention to these "routine" activities. A knowledgeable person can be quite effective under these circumstances in getting the council's position heard and not infrequently accepted at least in part. Members of the state legislature are probably better informed about where the council stands than are most clergy.

Only at one specific point on the question of race have the organized religious groups supported and maintained an office and a program that has a potential for far-reaching effects: Project Equality. Project Equality demands a commitment that the purchasing power of religious groups be used to support affirmative action on equal employment. It has had some measure of success, mostly at upper levels. Local congregations have taken part only on a limited basis. Yet Project Equality provides a model for "getting one's house in order."

With few exceptions, however, the leadership of the churches and the bulk of their membership have shown little insight into how to deal with the major problems of American society. Indeed they lack the tools, for the most part, for analyzing the problems. The very organizational patterns through which the ecclesiastical leadership is trained, recruited, and selected almost guarantees an "educated incompetence," an "occupational disability" for dealing with political issues.

This is not because there is no political activity within the Protestant churches. It is because even when politics takes place, as it does regularly, we have a host of euphemisms and disguises by which we deceive ourselves that we are not dealing with questions of power and privilege. The official recognition of different "parties" within organized religious groups continues to be frowned upon, no matter how much these differences are taken into account "unofficially." The ideology of consensus does not permit open recognition.

American Theology and Person-centeredness

On the question of social justice the self-deception is more deeply rooted than some defect of personality. The basic problem is theological. Protestant theology as it has developed on the American scene has generally been structurally inadequate to deal with the questions of institutionalized injustice. Our failure has been as much a matter of failure of mind as of a failure of heart.

There have been, of course, some glorious exceptions.

During the past generations the American churches have produced a number of major teachers of social ethics: the late Reinhold Niebuhr, his equally distinguished brother H. Richard Niebuhr, and my own pre-eminent teacher, James Luther Adams. These teachers and their successors are beginning to build a new body of American ethical theory vastly superior to most of what has come out of Europe. To these illustrious academic names must be added those of some remarkable practitioners of political ethics, particularly that of the late Martin Luther King.

Still it was not until the late 1950s that the number of teachers of Christian social ethics had grown to a sufficient number to warrant a professional society, the American Society for Christian Ethics. Even yet it is a fledgling among the professional societies to which religious professionals belong.

But the real questions are not the academic ones of the development of a body of ethical theory, of a tradition of social analysis, or the growth of a body of professional clergy competent to embody the ethic in parish ministry. The fact that from one point of view a fairly considerable number of clergy studied with these teachers does not guarantee that they caught their vision, nor that they successfully translated that vision into parish practice. Most of the best students went on to be teachers rather than parish clergy. The majority of the clergy in the parishes of America have taken their training in denominational seminaries, rarely even from the disciples of these great teachers.

What we have to remember is quite simply that for large numbers of parish clergy, both in their student days and in their ministerial careers, the courses in social ethics did not have the top priority. This is not where their chief interests lay; neither the organization of the parish ministry, with its structure of tasks, nor the organization of the typical Protestant religious group, with their program priorities, really demanded that ethics be a major priority.

Pastoral counseling, for very understandable reasons, got more attention. Nor is this concern for pastoral care in itself to be criticized or regretted; what is to be regretted is that in almost no seminary curriculum were any real relationships developed between pastoral care and social justice. In an adequate ministry they belong together; no social ethic should neglect the questions of personal wholeness. But in the seminaries, in the textbooks, and in parish practice, pastoral care and social concern often appeared to be exclusive alternatives rather than twin necessities.

But the study of ethics or its neglect does not tell the whole story. Formal ethical discussion is probably a minority preoccupation.

We need to look elsewhere and at different phenomena to understand the ways in which religion and politics affect one another. Patterns of Protestant morality that became dominant in the late nineteenth century still persist in many parts of the country. The emphasis in the churches, both middle class and working class, was fundamentally on personal ethics, personal development, whether this took the more moderate form of the undergirding of the virtues of Protestant respectability (for which the Prohibition campaign could serve as a prime example) or more emotionally intense insistence on "holiness." The stirring evangelistic campaigns of the nineteenth century, the national dominance of a Protestant morality which resulted in the Prohibition amendment, the ways in which an individual-centered code of conduct fit into the patterns of American public life during the decades from the Civil War to the Great Depression have left a remarkable and determinative residue of attitudes and beliefs among many Americans. The image of Protestantism which many intellectuals have, which shapes what is said in discussions of American history and American institutions, as well as in newspapers and periodicals, derives from this period of Protestant triumphalism. In addition through the Sunday school, through family indoctrination in religious and moral beliefs (where this continues), through radio ministries of many kinds, through the hymnody and devotional literature which local congregations use, this Protestant moralism continues to be reinforced. A person-centered Protestant Christianity persists—even among those who are not church members. Public stereotypes of what Christianity teaches also still reflect this "old time religion." Furthermore, as participation of many "liberal Protestants" in the McGovern crusade indicates, moralism is by no means limited to the "conservatives." One cannot really separate such issues as abortion, women's liberation, reform of sexually repressive legislation from structural considerations. But we must note that much of the rhetoric of reform is concerned with individual freedom, with questions of personal rights. Large elements of the "liberal" ethic remain as concerned with the individualistic focus as the conservatives; the differences lie in the answers, not in the problems. Furthermore the preoccupation with these questions remains in some measure a luxury platform for white middle class reformers; the changes proposed do not really strike directly at the graver issues of economic oppression.

"Watergate" can now serve as an almost perfect paradigm of the divorce of the personal and the social, of what happens when we separate official duty and personal morality sharply from one another. The paradigm is in fact so perfect as to seem a caricature. The Nixon Administration made a great show of its rigorous moral probity in private life, using "Law and Order" as the theme for a great moral crusade. John Ehrlichmann and H. R. Haldemann exemplified the apparently blameless private life—faithful husbands, dedicated fathers, church-going models of rectitude. Yet in public affairs these men and their associates could and did defend behavior which in the common judgment is immoral on the grounds of public necessity, "national security," and "reasons of state."

Here the chickens of Protestant moralism have truly come home to roost. It is small wonder, therefore, that Billy Graham, "the court chaplain" of this now discredited administration, lacked the theological and ethical tools to understand the nature of institutionalized immorality. A large number of devout Protestant clergy and lay persons no doubt find themselves equally at a loss that the public representatives of law and order could be architects of public disorder.

The "new morality" meanwhile turns out to be as person-centered and socially inadequate as the old.

What is striking, for example, in many of the discussions of the "new morality" is the extent to which these discussions fall into the domain of the pastoral counselors, not the social ethicists. Except for the structural aspects of women's liberation, concern with questions of sexual morality has had a personal-pastoral focus, not a socio-cultural one. Without question the issues have involved basic problems of personal relationships; without question too anxiety and anguish of a deeply personal kind have required attention to questions of personality formation, to processes of personal malfunctioning and reorganization, even to serious questions of identity. In all of this, we note first, however, that especially among those who became advocates of the "new morality" little by way of critical examination of the social roots of the new personality theories occurred, that few questions were raised about the underlying structural forces bringing about the social changes of which the "new morality" was a symptom, that the predominant values were often "personal growth," "personal freedom" without much concern for the social consequences of such a personalist orientation. Most of the conservative critics of the "new morality" were as personalistic as their opponents; they tended to accept the socio-economic status quo in the form of "the American way of life" without recognizing that social changes of many kinds were undermining these values. In their struggle against the immorality of "the consumer society" some conservatives fell prey to right wing reaction.

In a sense what was involved was a struggle between two kinds of pietism, the older traditional pietism, found among Protestants with a small town, old middle class and stable working class background (and among Roman Catholic traditionalists as well) and the newer psychological pietism, found in the newer middle classes, the mobile managers and suburban professionals, many of them among the customers of *Playboy* and similar publications.

For the most part neither advocates nor critics engaged in serious ethical reflection; their discussions remained at the level of "moralizing." The difference is significant, and it points to a major weakness in American religious thought. The moralist may of course engage in some serious analysis of an issue. We can find evidence for this in the literature which the temperance movement accumulated about "the liquor traffic." But the moralist does not ask questions about the assumptions on which his morality rests; he takes the authority of his position for granted. Nor does the moralist examine the structural bases, the sociocultural undergirding for the practices he is attacking. The Prohibitionist had little understanding of the social functions of drinking in Irish, German or Italian cultures, nor how the institutionalization of the use of alcohol in social ritual served to control abuse (more so in Europe than in the United States). The anti-Prohibitionist moralist of course also failed to ask questions about his assumptions; he did not ask why and among whom controls failed, what the socio-economic consequences of failure were, and so on.

Neither side looked at its anthropology, its understanding

of human nature, although at one level the failure of the two sides to understand one another was a function of two totally different understandings of what it meant to be human, of what sin consisted in, and how humans were to live before God. Further theological differences could also be explored, but are not germane to our main point: ethics is a critical and reflective activity; morality is not.

The lottery campaign can illustrate this quite clearly. For what is crucial in the prevalence of gambling is the implicit worldview, the hidden theology. The gambler's world is one where success and failure is a matter of chance; it is a world of caprice, "dumb luck", not one of predictable relationships of established order. Contrary to the Protestant ethic a great many Americans in fact believe that whether or not one is rich or poor is a matter of luck, not of deserving. "When my ship comes in," "when my number is drawn," and so on, I'll be able to escape from my present drab and confined condition. This view reflects the bitter experience of many middle class people as well as many of the poor. Hard work doesn't necessarily pay off, even if you're not black or poor to start with. Life is itself a kind of lottery to be faced with resignation, with a feast or famine mentality. Things can so quickly go bad.

Such a stance is of course not Christian, although many nominal Christians probably live by it. The stance reflects experience, reflects what in fact many families have known. Ethical analysis of the lottery issue would have revealed the necessity to deal with these problems and the structures of oppression they point to. Many families, including large segments of the presumably affluent middle classes, find little hope of advancement in their work, struggle hard to make ends meet, often with the help of a working wife or a moonlighting second job. But success and security seem as far off as ever. But the churches in their moralistic preoccupation with the lottery issue never came to grips with this underlying social reality.

As the campaigns against state lotteries illustrate, the typical

conception of the role of the churches and church members
in politics is that of officially organized ecclesiastical activity
run in and through the churches. Against such activity
parishioners of all political persuasions ought to protest on
theological grounds. *The place for politics is in the secular
arena; its proper vehicles are secular organizations.* This is
the point we made in the preceding chapter. In this chapter
we have come back to it again, but with a different agenda,
namely, with the intent of spelling out some of the parameters
of the concerns which a Christian political ethic must en-
compass.

The Nature of a Christian Political Ethic

A Christian political ethic will necessarily have its feet in
two worlds: the issues to which it will direct its concern will
arise out of the struggles that take place in a variety of public arenas; they will be problems arising out of our common
humanity. But the dynamic for the Christian ethic will come
from the Christian commitment to seek the neighbor's welfare. For the Christian this commitment comes out of the
experience of liberation which the encounter with Jesus as
the Christ has made possible, but it is at the same time *a
vision that the fundamental nature of the world is such that
the Christian ethic also must in the long run be the most
viable.*

What makes an ethic Christian regardless of the specific
directions in which some of its imperatives may point is always the commitment to Christ as Lord. A common loyalty to
Jesus Christ may nevertheless lead Christians of different theological persuasions to similar conclusions on moral issues. At
the same time, unfortunately, those with apparently the same
theological understandings do not always agree on moral
issues.

What these corollaries tell us then is that the route from
Christian commitment to specific moral decisions runs
through the fallible moral perceptions and commitments of

Christian believers. While our loyalties may be manifest, our duties are not.

At the same time the Christian ethic lays claim to realism. Insight into the realistic quality of the Christian ethic can come without any implicit appeal to the gospel. In an interview which he granted the *New York Times Magazine*, Kenneth B. Clark, quoting Bertrand Russell, appealed to "kindness" as the necessary ingredient for making school integration work. Clark did not mean to suggest that structural changes were irrelevant, but he did underline the fact that the learning climate of the classroom, specifically the attitude with which teacher approached students, must be considered a crucial variable. "Kindness" is basically an expression of a commitment to be concerned with the needs of the other, no matter who the other is. It is a recognition of the equal moral worth of all persons, not in abstract terms, but in the concrete style with which the other is encountered. Attitudes and structural change belong together; the evangelical impulse and social action dare not be separated. *Without love social action can become impersonally oppressive; without social action love can become sentimental and directionless.*

The claim that the Christian ethic is realistic is nothing other than the claim that the love of God informs the structures of human life, whether we are aware of this fact or not. This claim does not reduce the ethic to a secular code. Quite the contrary, for what the Christian wishes to proclaim through his witness is nothing short of the necessity to recognize the basic structure of the world in an explicit fashion; the claim is a translation of Luther's insistence in his explanation of the First Article of the Creed that God has not only created me and all that exists but that he also "out of fatherly goodness and mercy" sustains me, my fellow humans, and the entire creation. Furthermore, the dynamic of the Christian experience of liberation, to which the Second Article of the Creed testifies, supplies the motive power for the quality of concern for our neighbor that will keep new structural arrangements from deteriorating into old forms of exploitation.

Unless we see the world aright, unless we recognize that the power shaping the way in which the entire cosmos unfolds finds its human embodiment in the reconciling love which draws all humankind together into a single community, we do not have an ethic adequate to the tasks which we must carry out in this generation. To affirm the embeddedness of love in the cosmic process is, in one sense, simply to accept in the most comprehensive sense that all things do "work together for good for those who love God." We must take ownership of and accept responsibility for this kind of understanding and experience of the way things are.

The claim for realism rests first of all on the simple proposition that, as Luther noted, the love commandment belongs to the law not to the gospel. Put in another way, our interdependence can be experientially documented, rationally demonstrated, prudently supported. *Human survival requires the recognition of reciprocity.*

The ecologists provide the best contemporary documentation of the critical role which reciprocity plays in the survival of living forms. The basic context of morality is relational. This is why every purely individual-centered ethic will turn out to be inadequate.

But reciprocity has a double nature. Nowhere is this more interestingly documented than in one of the teachings of Jesus. "Do not judge, and you will not be judged yourselves; do not condemn, and you will not be condemned yourselves; grant pardon, and you will be pardoned. Give, and there will be gifts for you: a full measure, shaken together, and running over will be poured into your lap." Those injunctions find their rationale in the closing clause: "because the amount you measure out is the amount you will be given back" (Luke 6: 37-38; *The Jerusalem Bible*). For us as humans it is literally impossible to refrain from the activities here specified. To give them up would in fact be to give up moral action. What we need to recognize is the double set of possibilities inherent in what we do morally. For by our practices, by distrust, vindictiveness, niggardliness, we can set in motion a "vicious circle" that will have its consequences, as the Sinaitic teachings suggest, "to the third and fourth generation of them that hate me." But it is equally possible in the divine economy of grace to set up a virtuous circle, to set in motion chains of events that not only lead to human survival but to an improvement of the quality of life. Genuine mutual concern will build better communities than self-seeking individualism.

The concern for reciprocity, let it be emphasized again, is a matter of law not of gospel, of justice in our dealings with one another, not of unrequited and self-sacrificing love. What neither moral admonition, the reflections of social philosophers, nor even the efforts of the churches seemed to have communicated effectively has in our day become a central theme of all those concerned with the impending ecological catstrophe. In *The Limits of Growth*, whatever shortcomings in detail or in some of its assumptions we may find, we have overwhelming documentation of the complex interdependencies within which we exist. We belong together.

Perhaps, as many commentators believe, only the experience of far-reaching crises, of which we have a small foretaste in "the energy crisis" and the current inflation, will make us aware, even in a society so evidently committed to Christian beliefs as the United States, that we do in fact belong together. Our failure to recognize this simple truth, particularly in its truly comprehensive ecological form, must be a reminder how deeply the *incurvatus in se,* the turned-in-upon-self quality of much of our existence has eaten into what we think of as a Christian culture. In theological terms nothing could offer more convincing empirical evidence for the insight contained in the unpopular theological doctrine of original sin than the current documentation of the multi-dimensional catastrophes that threaten, the persisting conflicts among and within all the nations on this planet. This doctrine, despite some of the follies and inhuman cruelties perpetrated in its name (e.g. the eternal damnation of infants), has always served as a reminder of the self-destructive potential of the human species. The biblical story insists that it need not be this way;

the human species was intended for something better, indeed for an idyllic existence in mutuality with one another and all living things. But the record of human history to the present suggests that this self-conscious, tool-inventing, symbol-using species can also be the greatest destroyer of life, not its most creative expression. No one can read the somber literature of the ecologists without taking this possibility into account.

Human history, as well as our contemporary predicament, suggests that a considerable gap exists between human potential and actual performance. The recognition of reciprocity can itself be turned into lip-service. Even among Christians, as the *simul* reminds us, the preoccupation with self persists, can even be baptized and taken into the church. It is the Christian claim that the kingdom will come at the end of time beyond history. It is also the Christian claim that only the kind of transformation which death and resurrection symbolize can empower persons to live as the advance guard of the kingdom, as outposts, as colonists of heaven. What the law demands only the gospel can finally give; yet whether under restraint of the law or by the power of the gospel, we must recognize that we are in fact all mutually members one of another.

8

A CHRISTIAN POLITICAL ETHIC

We can now specify some of the basic elements in a Christian political ethic:

- A fundamental acceptance of the world of everyday affairs as the place where the life of faith is to be lived.

- The insistence that social justice is integral to the Christian life in every dimension of relationship and involvement; it is neither a luxury nor an option.

- The specification of a clear sense of direction in which a Christian political ethic must seek to move.

A Theological Basis

Behind these assertions, undergirding them, as already indicated, is a specific theological stance.

We need first, however, to look more closely at a particular problem that is often overlooked when theological foundations for social policy are articulated. The difficulty which most such explicit, generally biblically sound, theological positions encounter is that they often have little bearing on the working theology of parish pastors. I suspect that the major theological currents of the past generation carried less weight in the work of the parish pastor than the demands which rose out of the context in which he had to work and to pray, to preach and to counsel, to witness and to manage. The increasing academic excellence of theological education among the American clergy often resulted in a greater separation between theory and praxis. Too often the context which shaped the theory in the theological seminary was quite different from the context in which the parish pastor worked. The theology of the academy grew out of the intellectual quarrels of the theologians, out of the political, social, and ecclesiastical contexts in which they functioned; they provided few handles for understanding the contexts in which many clergy had to exercise their ministries.

We cannot really be surprised that the person-centered theologies of pastoral counselors, despite all the shortcomings those theologies had in the eyes of their more academically oriented theological professors, had more salience for many students and for many pastors. The counselors were after all reflecting, however uncritically in some instances, on the experiences pastors would encounter. They were giving them handles to understand their practice and to make that practice effective.

Reflection and experience belong together; too often the tools furnished in theological study did not fit the tasks which experience set. Pastors did not get a conceptual framework that enabled them to see the need for social policy as Christian witness within the contexts of their ministries: Only a handful caught in situations where oppression was blatant found themselves able to develop a theology that undergirded a social ethic.

"Doing theology" is an activity in which we seek to trace out what it means to live as Christians in particular places, involved in concrete constellations of rights and duties, opportunities and privileges. Doing theology means probing for the implicit credos by which persons run their secular enterprises and testing the adequacy of those credoes as bases for life-commitments. Doing theology means constantly exploring how the particular commitments one has made relate to one's ultimate faith-commitments. Doing theology in this way means uncovering what beliefs one is really willing to own, to live by and for, what beliefs really serve as the foundation for meaning, trust, and hope.

Effective theological analysis must be done with tools that enable clergy and laity alike to grapple effectively with the sociopolitical contexts within which they are living; it must be a theology that illumines the organizational settings, and above all, it must be a theology for which the reflective person can take ownership as providing guidance through the concrete decisions with which he is faced. The success of pastoral care often lay in the measure to which the clergy-counselors were able to accept and use pyschological language in a helping way; that they helped people was an important expression of their religious concern; that the language often reflected a different understanding of human behavior than the systematic theologians had taught them usually (until recently) led to a downgrading of theology rather than a wrestling with the intellectual task with which their experience confronted them.

The bureaucratization of ecclesiastical structures complicates in considerable degree the task of political ethics. This structure is itself an institutional framework that makes a holistic theology and an effective political ethic difficult. In today's ministry the demands which various ecclesiastical officials, boards, and commissions make focus on performance in the implementation of program; the theological content is implicit, highly conventional, and usually unexamined. Conformity to organizational directives, statistical achievement, and competence as a priestly functionary appear to have the highest priority. The bureaucratic reality of the church, the morphology of practice, proclaims a very different theology and a very different vision of the church than what is needed. The organization has its own message, and the message calls for maintenance rather than mission, for success rather than suffering, for the good old ways rather than the challenge of the new.

The gospel is not intended to serve primarily as an instrument of institutional perpetuation, even if the institution is the church. The gospel is a message to be proclaimed to the world. It is not amiss, therefore, to begin with a Christian understanding of the world. In particular, a theology that takes politics seriously must begin with the doctrine of the creation. Its initial assertion is that of a basic confidence in God and in the goodness of his care for the world.

There is nothing new about these assertions. Yet the moral preoccupations of conservative Christians have tended to let these fundamental propositions be forgotten. The primary theological reality with which we as humans must deal is not the fact of sin, individual and collective, but the fact of the goodness of God. To accept the doctrine of creation does not mean primarily to accept a set of propositions that detail certain procedural steps; to accept the doctrine of creation demands a particular set of attitudes towards the world which God made, that world which remains his world, the world in which he remains graciously active.

Thus we begin with the question about how Christians see the world, how they have been taught through tradition, through preaching and teaching, to experience the world. If it is indeed only "a vale of tears," if we do not see ourselves as in a fundamental sense a part of the world of creation, if we cannot experience the world in such a way that we can affirm its goodness, even in the midst of tragedy and disaster, then we end with a strange paradox. We not only deny the world, we not only see it as in some fundamental sense evil, but our ethical style of non-involvement carries a clear message: Either God wants it that way or else he is in fact helpless to change the world. That is, our non-involvement is in effect an affirmation of injustice, corruption, and tragedy as fundamentally the will of God.

What is being advocated here is not a set of new theological propositions but a different stance both in the education and in the ministry of the clergy; the new stance is both affirmative and relational. It accepts the world as the arena within which humans must live the life of faith and sees the pastoral task as one that takes seriously the sets of relationships (political, social, economic, ethnic, and so on) within which all persons must live. In the fullest sense we all live within communities that have natural, historical, and sociocultural dimensions. Doing theology in the parish is a way of reflecting systematically and from a particular perspective (the posture of faith) on the meanings found "in, with, and under" the experiential flow, routines and crises, which is our historical existence. How we act reflects what commitments we have made in particular communities. Theologizing seeks to make these commitments explicit.

The covert theologies with which many Christians operate are part of the agenda which must be examined. For example, the basic stance which many middle Americans take in their daily work may preach a louder message than the pulpit. For many of them the affirmation of the goodness of the world is not a matter of experience; instead, the world is a jungle, an arena of mortal combat in which only the few can triumph by dint of arduous and unrelenting effort. It's better to run scared, to be distrustful. It is also quite clear that those outside our own circle (whose radius may be quite small) need not be recognized as fully human. Whatever the good book says, the circle of Christian neighborliness does not run far beyond our own kind, our company of believers, or our ethnic community.

The theology implicit in this understanding of the world is as unchristian as the world of chance which is the worldview of the gambler. But the average pastor, let alone the average lay church member, has not learned to deal with theologies of this kind. He has sharply segregated his Sunday activities from his weekday occupation. He finds it difficult to look at the rules by which he runs his daily affairs and recognize in them crypto-theological assertions, to uncover his unspoken loyalties, let alone to call them into question. Since the pastor often shares more of these loyalties than he may consciously be able to admit, he may find ministry in situations of this kind extremely difficult. It is easier to let a perverse extension of total depravity read millions of fellow beings out of the human race than to challenge its proponents to a more adequate and critical understanding of the nature of theology and the radical implications of the gospel.

The affirmation of the goodness of the world, the basic confidence in God's care for the world, need not be a sentimental acceptance of the old liberal shibboleths. Indeed the liberal misapprehension of the depths of sin often had the same political effects as the conservative over-emphasis on the evil of this world: Neither took a good look at how the structural realities of the world actually operated.

It is the very presence of sin in the world that demands both individual compassion and organized efforts for social justice. Indeed the extent of injustice, oppression, and exploitation are such that organized efforts for social justice must have top priority. That is why a Christian political ethic is necessary.

But a Christian political ethic, no matter how necessary, would be futile without the presence of God's sustaining care in the world. Even in purely secular terms—apart from any concern for redemption—God cares for his world; God makes possible human survival, progress, the approximation of justice, the prevalence of peace, however fragile. The fundamental promise, "While the earth lasts, seedtime and harvest, summer and winter will not vanish from the world" testifies to those built-in processes by which the survival of this planet and of living forms, including human beings, is possible.

But a Christian political ethic goes farther. It believes that every human being is potentially redeemable; it knows from the gospel record that this redemption explicitly includes the outcasts, the wretched of the earth, the prodigals, "dregs from the alleyways and drug fiends pale," the ones farthest down.

If, for the most part, we have used the *simul* to remind us of the human propensity for evil, we need now to accent the assertion that the *simul* can equally be a reminder of the human empowerment to love, to seek justice, to serve the neighbor. The demand for holiness, as James Gustafson has noted, has its place in the Christian moral life. Whatever theological and ethical critique can be directed against a one-sided ethic of perfection, we must recognize the validity of the assertion that the life of faith should have the fruits of good works. Good works indeed ought to be "doing what comes naturally."

Because social injustice abounds in the world, we must have a social ethic that is as comprehensive as the world itself in its compassion; at the same time because we have a basic confidence in the goodness of God we know that compassion will make a difference, that social justice is attainable to a larger degree than now exists.

To begin with the doctrine of creation brings us to a second assertion important for a political ethic; we see the basic unity of the world despite all its diversity. To affirm this unity means to affirm the basic unity of humanity against all racist theories; to affirm the unity of the world means to affirm the interdependence of all parts of the world; to affirm the oneness of the world is to affirm our kinship with all living forms; our fundamental vision is ecological in the widest sense of that word.

A Christian social ethic must, in addition to this ecological vision, affirm the personhood of every human being. One can so easily formulate sweeping programs of reform in which the individual person becomes only a means to the program's end. As John Platt has recently pointed out, we must build not only on ecological vision but also on the affirmation of human potential, the understanding of the fundamental insights of existential philosophy, which in the age of scientific positivism, rescued personhood from disappearing in the impersonal processes of the cosmos. Ours is a world in which personhood belongs as an essential element; personhood, morality, indeed the existence of self-conscious valuing processes, the entire "third world" of the symbolic and the cultural belong together. Theology, philosophy, and indeed even science are only adequate interpretations of the world if they take all the data into account. The concern for social justice is a concern for the proper ordering of this "third world."

A theology that takes politics seriously must also have a doctrine of the church. Put with more particularity, it must have a doctrine of the gracious activity of God in human history. Though the proclamation of the Word God has called into being a company of those whom the Word has transformed; they are the people of God. The accounts of their origin are in the biblical record. They are a strange company—quarrelsome, divided, organizationally diverse. Their empirical forms are always fallible, subject to correction, sometimes to reformation root and branch. The organized religious groups, which call themselves churches are empirical exemplars, ways in which the people of God become visible in particular places and times. The basic test of their visibility is the presence of the Word in proclamation and celebration.

What does God intend through this strange company? Nothing less than that they are to be vehicles through which his will is expressed, given embodiment, communicated, in order that the kingdom his servants have proclaimed through the centuries may be brought to fruition. The people of God are the first fruits of the new creation; they are the exemplars of the life style of the kingdom; they are living witnesses to what God makes possible in the world.

These are, of course, very sweeping claims. They are nonetheless the claims which the biblical witness makes, the claims which in one way or another every generation has renewed. every generation has heard. In the imagery of the Revelation to John, the intentions of God are nothing less than a new heaven and a new earth. How this shall be possible we do not know in detail. In political life we can only deal with approximations, with the next step. Taking that step is difficult enough.

The Next Steps

As we move towards the end of the twentieth century it seems increasingly clear that genuine breakthroughs have occurred in the Christian understanding of how the will of God is working itself out. For the vision of the future must be global. Christians have of course always claimed that the entire world stands under the rule of God. The translation of that proposition has often been more imperialistic than evangelistic; the good news has altogether too often been accompanied by oppression.

The universality of the will of God must at the same time be accompanied by a sense of the particularity of its expression. A God who works in history must be understood in terms of the particular contexts, cultural, geographical, as well as temporal, in which his sovereignty is to be expressed. The result is a genuinely pluralistic vision, a vision that does not require that everyone speak with the same accent, understand the tasks of life from the same perspective, use the same rituals, the same forms of economic and social organization.

Such a pluralism could easily be asserted in the centuries when barriers of time and space kept peoples of different cultures widely separated. Today however we must assert pluralism in the context of continuing and increasing interaction. One consequence of our present situation is that we cannot afford a kind of laissez-faire relativism that lets every one do just as he pleases; for in an interdependent world the consequences may well touch the lives and fortunes of people thousands of miles away.

We must instead define the parameters within which genuine freedom and diversity are possible. Not everything goes. These parameters, which must be seen in dynamic interrelationships with one another, define the directions which are possible in our day; they define what the next step can be.

If the "liberation language" of oppressed people, as we hear it today, carries any meaning at all, the first of the values in terms of which directions must be determined is freedom itself. Freedom has many meanings in philosophical and religious writings. Here a very simple but essential human meaning is intended. *Freedom means that persons have genuine options; that the choices that lie before an individual are not just be-*

tween different varieties of the same basic kind. Freedom must be more than a formal legal concept; it must have substantive content. Such a definition of freedom is empirically testable; it has an operational meaning.

The concept of intrinsic control, which James Sellers uses, provides another insight into the meaning of freedom. Each person must have some significant social space within which initiative can be exercised. To be hedged in too closely by the demands of others, to be without elbow room to express one's basic self is to be unfree, regardless of apparent status or income. To be without significant choices whether in the marketplace or at the polling place, at work or at worship, is to be without genuine freedom. Diversity is a necessary condition for genuine freedom. This is why the search for a common denominator in American politics has so often trivialized the democratic process rather than enriched it.

A second value, equal in importance to the first, indeed always to be seen together with it, is equality. *Equality means the recognition of one's moral worth as a person along with other persons.* Equality does not mean standardization; it is not a quantifiable identity, although it has quantifiable dimensions.

The stress must fall on the combination of individuality with equality. Put otherwise, we must distinguish qualitative equality from quantitative identity. The black power advocates broke through to an important insight when they insisted that the struggles of black people for their rightful place, their genuinely equal place, in American society were not intended to make them indistinguishable from white people; their challenge has taken the definition of equality a step further, to be undeniably oneself, i.e., a black American, undeniably of equal worth to every other American. Such qualitative equality will be more difficult to obtain than standardized equality, than the interchangeable parts of a conformist assembly line, but it will also be infinitely more enriching.

A genuinely reciprocal society demands diversity. If we are all alike we have nothing to offer one another; we serve one another through our differences, but that service is best rendered under conditions of genuine moral and legal equality, in open transactions with one another.

These observations apply to women's liberation as well as to the black power movement. Nothing would be gained in achieving a society in which women were almost totally indistinguishable from men, or men from women. (Test tube babies could presumably almost totally erase the biological difference.) The demand for equal worth must be met; it must be met so that every woman is genuinely free to enter any social arena to which her aspirations and abilities direct her. Yet at the same time she should be free to affirm her sexual identity. So long as any woman cannot express her individuality in the pursuit of any occupation (no matter how much of a male monopoly it has been), both men and women will also not be free to pursue their individuality in the kinds of roles once traditional. Women will not be free to be mothers without a sense of betraying their sex, so long as they are not also free to be engineers; or to be both. Just what this may mean in a society in which qualitative equality is achieved must be left open. Experimentation and innovation will define for both men and women what shape equality combined with sexual identity will take.

Equality and freedom probably always exist in some degree of tension. For the pressures towards equality may well tend to limit freedom; some kinds of freedom must in fact be limited. On the other hand, the demand for freedom cannot help but set limits on certain kinds of equalization. To reduce all to the common norms of mediocrity may indeed achieve equality, but it has probably corrupted freedom.

Human beings have always had problems living with diversity. But the failure to accept diversity has led to dehumanization. "The hard hat revolt" against the apparent victories of black power, "victories" largely the creation of the immediate emotional impact of television news reporting, illustrates how in apparent self-defense we choose alternatives that perpetuate oppression both for middle Americans and for the struggling black minority.

Diversity cannot be imposed; creativity cannot be programmed. The resort to coercion will always be counterproductive, no matter how great the temptation may be to mount the final revolution.

We have much to learn about the conditions under which diversity and creativity will flourish; we have much to learn about what the moral practice of qualitative equality will be like. But the learning is going on, no matter how quietly. Qualitative equality requires an educational system in which all children receive attention in proportion to their needs, not their status. Equally important, quality education must include as an essential ingredient a personal teaching style and disposition that affirms the child as a human being.

It is this lack of the personal dimension that has made integration of schools so frequently a failure. Securing such moral commitment surely belongs on the agenda of the churches, especially since large numbers of public school teachers and administrators still belong to the church-going segment of American society.

If we can combine freedom and equality as here defined, we make possible genuine individuality. One of the major yet understandable threats to individuality can be found in the various movements for the liberation of minority groups in our day. In a genocidal situation it is quite understandable that advocates of black liberation charge those members of their group who do not find their values where the advocates do with being traitors. That is, in a battle for recognition genuine individuality may easily be suppressed. That is why the road to individuality can only run through the achievement of genuine equality and freedom. Where there is widespread recognition that ours is in fact a European-Afro-American culture not a transplanted European culture, genuine individual freedom and creativity will be possible.

Peace is a necessary condition for the achievement of these primary values. Peace means the development of mutual trust.

It is more than the absence of war. Peace in its fullest sense is *shalom,* the peace of God. In this sense every demand for peace is eschatological; it is a demand for the coming of the kingdom. No existing peace ever actualizes this demand, but the peace of the kingdom must serve as the controlling image for Christians to define the direction of their peace-making.

In this sense, as Stackhouse notes, the ecumenical efforts among the various Christian religious groups provide a prototype of the form the struggle for peace must take. Wherever Christians, whether through the World Council of Churches or through other international bodies learn to accept persons of differing traditions as brothers and sisters, we have a foretaste of the kingdom. Even beyond the bounds of the Christian community in relationships with other faiths, although the how and why of these efforts lie beyond the scope of this essay.

Two further parameters are of major importance. Whatever is done must be done within the limits of the resources of the planet earth, within limits that recognizes that these resources are finite, that they must be used with care, that they belong to the entire species. We must aim at such a care of the earth that it can sustain all of us without exploitation and without depletion.

Finally the pursuit of these values must take place within the framework of a sense of order. Order here again does not mean some international code or higher law imposed upon us, but the careful working out of the operations of our institutions so that administration has predictability; it means the rule of law, constantly tested in terms of justice, in terms of the preceding sets of values.

9

SOME POLICY ISSUES

It may be now possible to speak to certain basic issues.

Dealing with the structures of exploitation in society must come first. That is, in whatever program area we operate, we must deal with institutionalized racism and sexism. With the single exception of the passage of the equal rights amendment to the constitution, however, most of the work in dealing with these structures does not now call for sweeping legislation; it calls for implementation through administrative structures of the reforms already on the statute books. It calls, in addition, for tackling some of the indirect forces that undergird the structures of exploitation.

What we have learned (we should have known) in recent years is that however necessary legislation is, no statutes are self-enforcing. We need continuing pressure for affirmative action at every level—in government, business and industry, labor and education, in the professions and in housing; we certainly continue to need it in the churches. Laws are not self-enforcing. Without what James Sellers would call a supporting body of manners undergirding our statutes, our legislation is rendered null and void.

But we will never deal effectively with structures of exploitation unless we also deal with economic issues, specifically with the unjust tax burdens which fall particularly heavily on middle Americans.

George McGovern was unquestionably on the right track when he made tax reform a major campaign plank. Unfortunately the issue was muddied in several ways—both by his opponents and by the efforts of his own staff people to provide too many particulars in order to make a complex issue understandable. In the process several important elements were lost sight of.

First, Democratic politicians for understandable reasons did not like to admit that many of the reforms of the New Deal era did not really change the distribution of wealth in the United States to any great extent. Yet it is undeniably true that the gains which were made in the 1930s had limited effects. Furthermore, the New Deal never intended a sweeping transformation in American life. It was a rescue operation, not a revolution.

Second, because many liberals affirmed the New Deal uncritically, they did not see the new issues of the seventies. The New Deal did undergird the economic well being of large numbers of Americans. It would be impossible to think of auto workers, packing house workers, teamsters, steel workers and the like as among the elite of the American working classes had it not been for the New Deal. The New Deal made possible the present industrial labor movement; it undergirded not only its improved pay envelope but it also provided the machinery by which these workers won through collective bargaining some of the kinds of security for themselves that Social Security promised but did not actually deliver for many Americans.

The McGovern tax reform sounded like—its opponents saw to that—an attack on these hard-won securities. Many middle Americans were not ready to trust the government for their other securities—they were too aware of what Social Security and welfare really offered in contemporary America.

What is so easily overlooked in much that is written about "the welfare state" in the United States is the very limited extent to which the economic safeguards (Social Security, unemployment insurance, and so on) we have legislated actually reach. Not only does a considerable percentage of the labor force receive less than the maximum benefits (indeed the lowest paid workers receive far less than a decent minimum), but many workers, especially the least organized, are still uncovered. Only in the well organized industries do medical benefits reach a relatively satisfactory level. Many private pension plans offer the worker no benefits if his company goes out of business and no "portability" if he should change jobs. The "welfare state" has in fact bestowed greater benefits on the better paid white collar employees than on many blue collar workers, for whom the security was originally intended. Thus many blue collar Americans have good reasons to be distrustful of some of the reforms which politicians have offered them.

Even before the present inflation made the lot of many "average Americans" more difficult, these persons had learned that despite reforms, despite the promises of the politicians, life remained undeniably difficult — it was hard to stay ahead of the bills, hard to hedge against the possibilities of serious illness, hard to partake of the promise of American life, despite the blandishments of the TV commercials, the propaganda of the Chambers of Commerce, or the awareness that millions of others, both black and white, were worse off.

It remains true that the present tax system—national, state and local—offends against equality, that it subsidizes the wealthy at the expense of the poor. The consequence, however, is not only an offense against the poor; it is equally an offense against freedom and individuality. The "little people" cannot be blamed for their distrust of big government, big business, glib politicians, and rich people.

We must add that the tax system does not protect resources from depletion; it fosters a war economy and an economy of waste, not an economy of abundance. It does not undergird either freedom or equality.

To get at the problems of tax reform requires a broader strategy; it will require the development of alternative institutions to the military-industrial-educational complex that has developed over the last quarter century.

One point must be emphasized. It seems simple enough. The major barrier between the poor and the rich is not "the culture of poverty"; it is not the lack of motivation; not the gobbledy-gook of the welfare imperialist. It is quite simply money. To put money into the hands of the poor with the fewest possible strings is, I suggest, a major part of the solution. It will help the broken black family stay together; it will make all kinds of meaningless values become meaningful.

The test for this proposition is quite simple: a comparative study of the attitudes of those who receive income payments in ways that are considered respectable, even though these payments do not come as wages for work (although they have been earned) with those who receive welfare payments. Compare the older person on Social Security with the one drawing old age assistance; the worker drawing supplementary unemployment benefits with the one getting public assistance. Compare the difference which amount of income makes in terms of various kinds of societal adjustments. I do not mean to suggest that money is the solution to all problems; but money does allow humans to have the freedom to deal with certain kinds of problems. Without money it makes no sense even to try one's strength against other problems.

Proposals for the negative income tax, for family assistance (the Nixon administration effort), for guaranteed incomes can end the present paternalistic atmosphere in which some welfare families may do better than the non-welfare poor, but in which many persons become pauperized, and almost all find that welfare puts their privacy at the mercy of personally well-intentioned yet frequently arbitrary welfare professionals.

It will of course remain true that even with these reforms some of the poor will remain obnoxious, ungrateful, disorganized in their personal habits, just as some rich people are. Personal reform is not the first business of government; the issue is not separating the "deserving" from the "undeserving" poor. Even in the rehabilitation of criminals, from the viewpoint of public policy, the crucial question is not whether the "moral character" of the criminal has been transformed but simply whether the likelihood of the continuation of criminal behavior is reduced more effectively by "rehabilitation" than by "punishment."

With money in their pockets the poor should be free to go into the market to purchase their needs, just as the rest of us do. Their needs may include the necessary "psychological" services from private agencies under the same terms of confidentiality which the rest of us can take for granted. Too often today public social services serve the purposes of their professional staffs more effectively than they serve the needs of their clients. Because the clients are not free, because they have no intrinsic control over their own space, they are at a disadvantage. They lose not only freedom; they usually do not gain anything from the proffered help. They are double losers. But they do not have to be.

A second major area for political reform is taming the large bureaucracies that have developed in our day. These bureaucracies are by no means just political; nor are numbers the only criterion. A small school system, given the conformist mentality of school administrators, can be as oppressive as a large office. Bureaucracy is a prime example of the operation of hierarchy, often without collegial accountability. Thus bureaucracy offends against equality, freedom, and individuality.

Bureaucracy, as Max Weber pointed out, is rule-dominated. The development of rational procedures is part of the achievement of administrative predictability. It is also a way of fitting round pegs into square holes. Bureaucracy thus offends against personhood; it is the very incarnation of the false dichotomy between person and office.

Many Americans, especially the better educated ones, operate with the benign assumption that established procedures in administrative matters, especially if the office-holders are in the civil service, are objective and impartial. This notion is implicit in the ideal of a "government of laws, not men." These persons forget to ask in whose favor the rules have been made and in whose behalf they are enforced. But in every bureaucratic decision someone wins and someone loses; whether such an outcome is just or unjust is not simply a matter of whether the decision was made according to the rules but it is also a matter of the substantive content of the decision. American industry has known the importance of getting the "right administrators into the regulatory agencies." Management knows the power inherent in the authority to formulate and to interpret administrative rules. It is no accident thus that the chief supporters of "non-partisanship" in government, especially on the local level as the city manager system so well illustrates, come from the "right side" of the tracks. City managers are, of course, primarily administrators, but an administrative practice *consistently followed* constitutes policy just as much as any directive which an elected city council has voted. The myth of bureaucratic impartiality is a part of the larger myth of our times, the myth of "disinterested knowledge," one now heavily under attack in both political and scientific circles.

The experience which many average Americans, as well as the poor, have with bureaucracies, public and private, not only "proves" to them that they are powerless to cope with "the system" but also that those who hold power are basically unsympathetic with the poor. Ironically, among the most powerless, are the lower echelon employees of many of the bureaucracies, especially some of those with considerable education. Public school teachers, for example, must be counted among the victims of educational administrators at the same time that many of them inflict similar impersonal injury on the children in their classrooms. From one point of view, especially for those who are "conformity-oriented" rather than "self-directed," doing one's job by the book is the path of least resistance.

The problem of bureaucratic impersonality will not be easy to solve. Two directions are suggested: the decentralization of the bureaucracy to prevent the constant buck-passing up the chain of obstruction, and the development of guidelines that stress personhood and self-initiative as primary criteria in the enforcement of bureaucratic rules, with effective delivery of services as a major test. We must ask welfare administrators to talk about the number of persons they have helped rather than the number of dollars saved. In the end they will also save more dollars.

Without question bureaucracies are necessary; they can be a highly efficient piece of societal technology, especially where routine repetition of certain tasks makes up a dominant part of an organization's activities. But all bureaucratic operations need to be constantly scrutinized for the humane quality of their performance. Watchdog organizations are essential.

Political parties provide one kind of watchdog organization: a client who feels mistreated can frequently get an advocate in the local party organization. Unfortunately the very poor seldom use this route; in most cities efficiently functioning political clubs are no longer found in many of the neediest neighborhoods. Too many of the persons seeking favors may also turn out to want help that is not legally theirs. Nevertheless parties do operate to humanize bureaucracies.

The press can also serve a watchdog function. By and large, however, the press does not have the manpower to give adequate coverage. Furthermore, by the nature of journalism, press coverage will more frequently lead to surveillance of public rather than of private bureaucracies. Private voluntary agencies will have to carry a good deal of the burden. On the national scene Ralph Nader's organization has provided some of this kind of help, although by and large Nader's interests lie elsewhere. Civil rights groups, women's liberation organizations, labor unions, consumer groups, environmental groups, and the like are already doing much of this work. More needs to be done.

Another alternative that combines decentralization with a highly efficient delivery system involves the use of private organizations locally based with a contractual or purchase of service arrangement with a public agency. Neither of these concepts is new; indeed some of the same problems of bureaucracy and impersonality can arise in these settings. What large scale bureaucracies, public or private, profit or non-profit, often lack are structures that provide some accountability to the community where the service is rendered, that have some local power base to enable them to deal with the superordinate authorities on more equal terms. Where staffing and direction are local, although standards of performance are set externally, and where the local community must provide some of the resources, both the local community and the superordinate agency have ways of making their demands and needs felt.

Neither this formula, nor any other necessarily guarantees increased sensitivity to the people served. Public education, in fact, illustrates some of the basic weakness in the proposed model of decentralization. Two major reasons quickly suggest themselves for the shortcomings of local control of public schools. Generally speaking, we cannot in most local communities locate any citizen's group that exercises a persistent watchdog function, that provides a political constituency to which school board members are accountable and on which they can rely for support. School board members, like members of city councils in non-partisan city manager situations, often find themselves alone; they are faced with responsibilities that require more time than they can give for the nominal remuneration they receive, and in effect depend upon the educational administrators for information, technical guidance, and for what little critical input they get on policy questions. Doing an effective job becomes extremely difficult under these circumstances.

In the second place most school board members (as well as city council members in the city manager system) soon discover that the professionals are well organized, have a fairly clear conception of what they want, and in most cases effectively control the one citizen organization that presumably has a long-run interest in the schools, the PTA. There are, of course, notable exceptions, where PTAs have functioned independently, often in opposition to the school board as well as the administrators.

The objection that this proposal would "politicize" education, as some persons might interpret the above analysis, misses the point that an implicit political control already exists; by default the administrators have taken power into their hands or a small, often inconspicuous citizen group is running affairs and determining policy. The answer to the tyranny of the few is obviously not to reduce citizen participation but to increase it many times. Just as the answer to excessive centralization is to bring decision-making discretion to the lowest policy echelon in the hierarchy.

What is missing in most bureaucracies and in non-partisan structures is clear-cut *accountability to the public*. Without such accountability arbitrariness can flourish without effective challenge. Political parties provide an important although imperfect structure of accountability.

Public education in most communities reflects not only the sluggish responsiveness of the bureaucrat but the lack of effective alternatives for most children. Provided one could get over some of the emotional hang-ups and continuing religious animosities about parochial schools, this model would provide at the level of elementary and secondary education some meaningful choices among alternative systems for the children of middle and lower income Americans, choices that the well to do enjoy now. This proposal does not mean providing money for the pseudo-private school developed — even under religious sponsorship — to avoid racial integration. Tax monies should not subsidize evading the spirit as well as the letter of the law. The proposal does suggest, however, that we need to re-examine to what degree our defenses of "separation of church and state" are polite forms of anti-Catholicism (not quite erroneously described as the anti-Semitism of the intellectuals) rather than genuine resistance to the establishment of religion. The unofficial "civil religion" of many Americans, including some of the ideologists of "separation," seems to me a much more dangerous establishment than any of the explicitly religious groups would ever dare to attempt.

Nevertheless the use of "mixed" models, private agencies under contract or receiving program grants, with local policy-making boards needs further exploration, especially in health care and in the various therapeutic services. The concern of government should be with the enforcement of basic criteria of performance. Government could then properly evaluate results, i.e., the number of persons effectively helped. A diversity of approaches, while threatening to some professionals, might well uncover new ways of bringing help to persons in need. The welfare bureaucracy has shown little by way of results in dealing with the human problems that are often found in poor families. The combination of governmental coercion, inquisitorial tactics, and administrative restraints often give public agencies an inescapable antagonistic posture over against their clientele. Traditional attitudes towards the poor are easily perpetuated, indeed reinforced. A new and more experimental approach as already illustrated in some community mental health programs, may be the proper prescription for success.

Two points must be underlined. Obviously the current hostility between private and public welfare must be overcome. This also means a basic re-examination of the priorities of most united funds. Not only do these funds often represent institutionalized racism and sexism at their worst, but they also tend to perpetuate agencies based on past needs and are very slow to provide ample support for agencies dealing with newly discovered needs, perhaps because these needs are often controversial. The laggard response of most united funds to the needs of agencies serving black people can easily be documented; the National Urban League has time after time been forced to subsidize new programs with large grants of money from sources outside of united fund channels. The timidity of united funds in supporting family planning agencies is a national scandal. The ideology of consensus, of not rocking the boat, has been particularly virulent in the power structures of private philanthropy.

The development of a complex of alternative peacetime institutions to counter the military-industrial-educational complex will be a more difficult operation. We shall not undertake this task unless we recognize not only the existence of the military-educational-industrial complex but also the extent to which this complex has determined the imperialistic foreign policy we have followed for many years. Here critics from both the extreme right and the extreme left have provided documentation which the scholarly community, the literary intelligentsia serving as a priesthood molding American public opinion through their journals and publications until the coming of the Vietnam war, has conveniently dismissed. We need an effective alternative to this destructive complex which has far too long had too large a voice in defining national policy.

Several premises ought to be obvious to Christians as well as to all humanitarians. Our foreign policy must be based on taking seriously the proposition that citizens of other countries are of equal worth with our own. This strikes deep at national ethnocentrism, at American "manifest destiny" mentalities. But it must be done.

We are still far from recognizing the need for an effective alternative in our national policy-making. The imaginative use of private agencies in international assistance might help us deal with some of the worst features of the present foreign aid programs, namely, that they are often developed to support an imperialistic American foreign policy (shoring up oppressive regimes all over the world), that too often economic aid gets sucked into the foreign policy trough, that much of it in addition does not reach its destination but lines the pockets of local "beneficiaries." Private agencies — especially many of the church agencies — have a much better track record.

A new kind of program surveillance would also be possible. Today it is in the interests of administrators to cover up failures; it is equally in the interests of "beneficiaries," especially when they represent vested interests to cover up the misuse of aid programs. In a purchase of service or contractual arrangement with private agencies, the government would have a strong interest in getting a dollar's service for a dollar paid. In addition the constituencies of the private agencies, having themselves a basic interest in the objectives of the aid program, might well subject their own administrators to continuing scrutiny (as is well illustrated in the work of the church agencies). New constituencies, the possibility of experimental programs, the opportunity to enlist volunteers — these would provide new inputs of energy into foreign aid. Actually some of the community development programs of the Lutheran World Federation, as well as those of other groups, already illustrate this new model.

An arrangement of this kind would not eliminate politics. But some kinds of political manipulation would undoubtedly be reduced. At the same time the churches would be forced (by the American principle of separation) to keep these agencies organizationally independent. One danger of the arrangement could be a too cozy relationship between churches and government; institutional safeguards would have to be developed.

What I am asking for is a new set of national priorities.

I am not asking for a new set of political slogans. I am as tired as most American critics of "New Frontiers," "Great Society" and other capsule definitions. We are still trying to meet the future with sleight-of-hand tricks. The job is much, much more difficult.

Put simply, economic realities call for a service economy. Working out what this means in particular industries will require the imagination and energy of thousands, tens of thousands. No single piece of legislation will do it.

Economic realities call for realistic care for the poor and the handicapped. I have tried to suggest some beginnings. Much more will need to be done.

Economic realities call for bringing certain disruptive forces under control — to take a careful look at the role of property, planning, the use of environments, to look at the transportation problem; at the idea industries.

None of this suggests that we need to give up an economy based on "profit and loss." Profit is not a dirty word, but profit must be related to service; service must be independently evaluated. The profits of pornography are, for example, a horrible example of what our society will tolerate. We can also be reasonably sure that the biggest money-makers will be the ones safest from prosecution. It will be the little people who will go to jail.

Developing a sense of direction is essentially a matter of theological and ethical stance. But theological and ethical stances must be spelled out in detail, in programs for particular times and places.

10

BEYOND POLITICS AS USUAL

Conservative Christians may well wonder whether the argument up to this point has not proved too much. If the proper arena for the Christian exercise of compassionate concern for the neighbor is the secular world with all its ambiguities, compromises, and surrenders, and the preferred agency is some voluntary association for social reform, an interest group, or a political party, has the Christian witness any distinctive quality of its own? Is there no place for Christians to draw the line in a way that marks them as uniquely obligated?

The problems of hierarchy and collegiality, of authority and freedom, are general problems, by no means distinctive of ecclesiastical organizations as such. The dialectical tension to which the *simul* points may sometimes appear to be little else than the recognition that no aspirations, no ideals are ever without self-interest and that no achievement ever lives up to its original promise. Human performances always fall short of their projected goals.

But the Scriptures apparently make a stronger claim. The passages of the Bible which have ordinarily been employed in the development of a Christian political ethic which have generally been Romans 13:1-7 (Let every soul be subject to the higher powers. — KJV) and Matthew 22:21 (Render unto Caesar. . . .) Traditional interpretations of these texts have defined the political stances of most Christians for many centuries. Accepting the voice of tradition as correct, most Christians gave little attention to the possibility that the texts might be understood differently.

God and Caesar

The basic Christian claim, the evident source for the dualism of empire and papacy, church and state, surely is rooted in the distinction between what belongs to God and what belongs to Caesar. After all Jesus himself drew this line clearly enough.

Christians unhappy with the traditional stance yet faithful to the biblical texts have not usually chosen to question these texts but to set other texts against them. The book of Acts provides the famous and frequently quoted, "It is better to obey God than man." The Revelation to John provides not so much further proof texts for exegetical debate as an apparently totally different perspective on the nature of the state, namely, its embodiment of the anti-Christ, the demonic. Christians highly involved with the more esoteric prophetic literature have had ample opportunity to interpret contemporary troubles in terms of biblical prototypes.

One preferred solution has been to withdraw from the public arena. Such withdrawal has not put an end to political structures. Without the protection which these structures have provided, sometimes quite explicitly, sometimes more indirectly, these groups could not continue to exist. More seriously, their withdrawal implies a defective theology of creation. The stance of withdrawal on the basis of the inherently contaminating quality of political life implies that in large measure, if not totally, the earthly community, the realm of Caesar, is in fact also the realm of Satan. One may conclude that in effect God has surrendered the largest part of his creation to the domain of evil. The two cities are those of God and Satan.

The temptation to equate the heavenly community with one's own religious enclave (no matter how miniscule) and all other communities (the rest of human kind) with the domain of Satan has, of course, a kind of Scriptural warrant. More than one of the leading theologians of the church, including Augustine, has spoken in this way. Luther's writings, especially some of his earlier tracts, also contain language of this kind, as if the proper dichotomy in the world were the one between believers and unbelievers, and all other dichotomies were simply derivative.

The data at hand for determining an issue of this kind are obviously mixed. Scriptural language and theological tradition both provide some warrant for this rigid separation of the washed from the unwashed. Notions of double predestination add a final metaphysical warrant. Yet scriptural, theological, and ethical grounds also exist for the rejection of this position. The detailed arguments will not be marshalled here, but an understanding of the doctrine of creation, of the universalistic impetus found in later prophetic writings as well as in the gospels, and particularly a fuller understanding of what "love of neighbor" implies provide the kinds of counter-arguments that can be used. The metaphysical dichotomy finally dehumanizes; it runs counter to the desired ethical outcome of the preaching of reconciliation, the new being in Christ, humanization.

Theocracy seems the only participatory position consistent with rigid dualism. The theocratic impulse, despite the fact that its response to the world apparently opposes the counsel of withdrawal, really rests on the same judgment about the world. Unless the saints rule, the structures of our worldly existence are under the domain of Satan.

Theocracy seems a simple enough position. The establishment of a truly Christian state is an appealing goal. Difficulties nevertheless abound. Not only must one determine who belongs in the company of the saints, i.e., who is truly entitled to rule — depending upon the laxity or the stringency of one's criteria, one can end up either with an inconsequential minority or with an almost nondescript aggregation of the passably righteous — but one must also determine the standards by which the theocracy shall be organized.

The history of the Prohibition movement provides profitable reading on this question; we cannot totally ignore how much of the success of this crusade rested on deals with politicians who drank one way and voted the other. But Protestants were so busily engaged in establishing a "Christian America" that most of them apparently took little note of the compromises they made along the way. The determination to "establish righteousness" obscured the lessons in practical politics which the churches might have absorbed from the Great Crusade. Covering the ambiguities of the pursuit of power with the cloak of righteousness, the proponents of public morality denied how muddy the road to success actually turned out to be. The virginal innocence of their cause was not to be sullied.

Both withdrawal and theocracy are essentially sectarian responses. They require their practitioners to exclude large numbers of Christians from the company of the righteous. But so long as the dualism, which has dominated Christian thought and practice since the Constantinian establishment, remains we will see sectarian responses of these kinds. This dualism has been determinative of a great deal of Christian political ethics. The proper response to it is to recognize that our century has seen the conclusive end of the Constantinian era.

The end of the Constantinian era can be noted in three separate but equally important developments, all of them associated with one of the major instances of religious resistance in our century, namely, the struggle of a segment of the German Christian community, both clergy and laity, against Nazi tyranny, a struggle which as the Barmen Declaration makes so clearly evident found the resources for its strength both in a renewed understanding of the biblical word and in a reappropriation of the traditions of the sixteenth century. The Bible and the Reformers, particularly in Protestant circles, had something to teach the faithful of the twentieth century.

The Reassertion of Divine Sovereignty

The first important development in Germany was the reassertion of divine sovereignty over all of life. I have deliberately put this proposition in language more familiar to Calvinist than to Lutheran theologians. Barmen was a cooperative venture; ecumenical in the most proper sense, that is, a calling together of Christians on the basis of the Word of God itself. It is furthermore significant that one of the important authors of the Barmen declaration was a Lutheran, Hans Asmussen, whose theological explication of the basic articles of the Barmen statement the synod made a part of its official declaration.

All political authority is derivative; only the divine authority is original. All political authority may in the proper context be called into question. To assert a proposition of this kind is simply to return to the authentic reformation tradition, Lutheran and Calvinist. For whatever the two kingdom proposal of Luther did or failed to do, it never at any point intended to suggest that political authority was autonomous. Both kingdoms in Luther's understanding of them were "under God."

There can therefore be no question whatsoever of the right of religious spokesmen, clerical or lay, to call political authority to account. The question of when or how this is proper needs careful examination, but the existence of the right, the obligation in fact, is and must be unquestioned.

The Secularity of Politics

The second consequence of the German Church Struggle, therefore, although perhaps not made fully explicit at the time of the Barmen declaration, is the insistence that political life belongs to the realm of the secular. Two denials are involved in the assertion of the secular nature of politics. First, very specifically, the entire cult of throne and altar, the aura of divinity protecting all in authority, must be called into question. All remnants of any "divine right" to rule must be extinguished, whether in hereditary princes or in elected chief magistrates.

The lessons of the church struggle have not been adequately learned, either in Germany or in the rest of the Christian world. We must not forget that the alliance between nationalism and piety is an old one, found almost wherever organized Christianity has been a dominant influence in the history of a nation. The powerful always like to claim that God is on their side.

The affirmation of the secularity of political institutions also establishes their relativity, i.e., calls into question any sanctification of the status quo. This second consequence moves us one step beyond resistance: resistance can be justified simply on the basis of the perverted performance on the part of an otherwise acceptable political authority. But if institutions are themselves inherently relative, it is also proper under certain circumstances to change them, even to change them radically. Leaving aside the metaphysical assumptions inherent in the Declaration of Independence, the principle of the relativity of institutions asserts nothing other than the Declaration's principle that the people may change their governments.

Before we look at the sweeping nature of this statement with respect to political institutions, we ought to realize that the assertion of the secularity of institutions and their attendant relativity applies to all institutions, not just to political ones. For a sociologist there is nothing surprising in a statement of this kind; he may also add that the number of options open for solving certain persistent human problems is actually quite limited; advocates of sweeping change frequently discover an almost massive inertia in large-scale institutions; existing practices presumably have an evolutionary survival value that must not be overlooked. None of these responses will, of course, satisfy the theologian, particularly if he is a conservative thinker. He will ask for at least some kind of biblical warrant.

The biblical warrant is easily available, although it has been generally ignored. Nowhere do the biblical writings prescribe a particular pattern of institutional organization. Certainly they contain no political blueprints, for the political organization of the ancient Israelite and Judaic kingdoms itself changed over the centuries. Christian ecclesiastical organization no only differs from the forms found in the Old Testament, but the diversity of Christian opinion suggests strongly that the New Testament contains no unequivocal directives. Similar observations apply to family and economic organization. The constants of the biblical witness are not organizational constants.

The biblical constants are human constants. "The Sabbath was made for man," Jesus replied to his critics, "not man for the sabbath." Thus he challenged one of the most sacred religious practices of his day. Put in more general and contemporary language, we may say quite simply: *Institutions exist to serve human beings; humans should therefore not be sacrificed to institutional forms.* In the language of the Declaration of Independence, "to secure these rights, governments are instituted among men."

LuVern V. Rieke, professor of law at the University of Washington, has recently made the same point in commenting upon legal systems. "Even though the theologians," Rieke writes, "might concur with Luther's statement that man could alter even the decalogue (reading sabbath as Sunday instead of Saturday is either an amendment or an interpretation which ignores firmly established precedent), any announcement to that effect would be received by the church-going public with about the same understanding and enthusiasm accorded Christ when he commented upon the subservience of the sabbath to man."

"The point is," Rieke adds in the next paragraph, "that the legal system cannot do its job if the *rules,* whether promulgated in or out of Scripture, are regarded as holy." Political institutions, moral rules, legal norms are all subject to change.

Romans 13

These are far-reaching statements in the light of the customary interpretations of Romans 13. They involve not merely questioning conventional interpretations of this passage but also the Barthian revision. While I am not interested in getting into an exegetical debate, some comments on this passage are nevertheless necessary.

Otto Dibelius, for many years the remarkable Lutheran Bishop of Berlin, in a little work on the meaning of the German word for government, *Obrigkeit,* undertook the demythologization of the key term in the German Lutheran ideology of obedience. Although our situation is different from that which he faced, not only under Hitler but in his difficult post-war circumstances as well, and although we need not agree with every inference he draws from his reexamination of Luther's understanding of Romans 13, his reflections are nevertheless very instructive for us.

Dibelius performed two very different tasks in his little book. He pinpointed first of all the influence of a tradition of interpretation going back to Luther, namely, Luther's patriarchal extension of the meaning of "obedience to father and mother" to include magistrates. Generations of German children memorized Luther's words as part of their religious instruction. Generations of religious teachers, pastors, and theologians buttressed Luther's interpretation with further citations from his work: the *Large Catechism* and other writings.

But the real damage, Dibelius contends, came in Luther's reading of Romans 13:1-7. The point which Dibelius makes about these verses as constituting an interruption of Paul's argument in chapters 12 and 13 can be disputed. But the thrust of his argument is worth noting. These verses reflect an understanding common in the Mediterranean world of the first century that a cosmic order undergirded the existing institutions. The world in its constitution has a moral order. God has arranged matters in this way. Transgressing this moral order brings sanctions. It constitutes a framework within which the forces at work in the cosmos are restrained. The Roman empire exemplifies this order in its legal traditions. Relating to this order is not a matter of obedience; it is a matter of acceptance, of getting in step with the nature of things. Thus the admonition is a general one — addressed to every soul, not only to Christians; it has nothing to do with obedience as such.

Luther misread the passage, so Dibelius argues (persuasively so far as I am concerned) in terms of the political arrangements of his day. Luther's German rendition of the original as *Obrigkeit*, i.e., the ruling body, the authorities, describes a much more particular political institution than "higher powers" or "the powers that be," the translation found in the English and Swedish Bibles. Thus implicitly he bestowed a divine sanction on the historically contingent. His interpretation put the emphasis on political passivity.

Two American writers have recently addressed similar questions, although from very different perspectives. In *The Politics of Jesus* John Henry Yoder calls for a radical messianic understanding of Jesus. John Sellers in *Public Ethics* makes a case for active citizenship, for "willed initiative." In his judgment freedom from extrinsic control over both personal and communal space is an abiding American moral tradition. The struggle continues down to the present day; it demands an active citizenship committed to the common good. While Dibelius is working on a different agenda, he nevertheless points out that the changes in human political arrangements which have come with popular participation in political decisions have rendered the old political ethic inapplicable. Today's world calls for an involved citizenry.

The Demand for Active Citizenship

Is citizenship to be understood primarily in active or in passive terms? For Sellers, the active understanding seems rather uniquely related to American institutions and American history. It seems to me more proper to argue that active citizenship belongs to the understanding of human nature appropriate to institutions of self-government wherever they appear. Active citizen participation is a necessary condition for healthy self-government. It represents the live option of current history.

In a complex and interdependent world active involvement cannot be limited to one sector of our common life. What needs to be underscored is that in a particularly striking way human beings have become the "creators" of their own social institutions. The human social order is in certain senses a humanly constructed world.

Actually this has always been true. The propositions that social institutions are contingent, relative, and products of human efforts belong together. Whether he takes a historical perspective, in which he sees how social changes, including sometimes sweeping changes in social organization, follow as the consequences of human initiative—whether in the form of political conquest, technological discovery or invention (e.g. the mechanization of agriculture), religious reformation and revitalization (the Mohammendan conquests), or whether he chooses a longer evolutionary perspective, in which he looks at question of selection and adaptation, the student of human society sees societal forms as the result of collective human effort within the limits set by biological and physical givens.

On biblical grounds we can make a further assertion. Isador Chein has recently pointed out in an entirely different context that the creation account in Genesis actually suggests that the task of continuing the work of creation has been specifically assigned to human kind. Calling on an old Jewish teaching, he sees humans as partners with God in the creative process. Here he finds the essence of the divine image. Seen in the larger context of partnership in "the care of the earth", we have here an understanding of the human task that can be applied to many areas of life, not least of all in the political arena.

The Limits of Politics

To be called to active participation, against the background of the German church struggle and the reflections of Bishop Dibelius, brings into focus the third major contribution of the 1930s: the recognition of the specific yet limited role of political institutions in the service of human needs. Humans are not to be subservient; they are to be active participants; but their participation is not to erect sacred empires; it is to serve the needs of their neighbors and of the entire creation.

In a more striking fashion, in the very midst of the German church struggle, Martin Niemöller, preaching on the classical locus of dualistic political ethics, Matthew 22:21, made it crystal clear that we must constantly remind Caesar that his claims are limited claims. There is no separate and autonomous realm of the political that is free of divine judgment. Put in more secular and political language: no realm of political activity can claim exemption from ethical scrutiny; none can claim absolute loyalty; none is above criticism.

The results of such a stance will be twofold. First of all, it is only by the restriction of the political, by drawing a clear line that establishes its limits, that the freedom of the gospel can be maintained, that the sovereignty of God can be actualized. Second, affirming the validity of the secular isn't a carte blanche for the politicizing of salvation—all political programs must constantly be seen within the limited contexts of what is politically appropriate. In fact we must not allow any one institution to dominate all others.

We have seen in American life the terrible effects of allowing the mentality of the marketplace to play a dominating role in the shaping of our institutions; in a consumer society obsessively driven to ever greater production of commodities of all kinds, the hucksters have found ways to translate the values of almost every sphere of life into commercial terms: sex, athletic prowess, piety, artistic gifts, teaching skills, all have been sucked into the all-devouring maw of the American economic system. The tyranny of the market over all facets of our lives must be questioned; many of the young have done just this, perhaps with more romanticism than realism, but nevertheless with the right instincts.

We must not allow political tyranny to step into the place of an economic one. The ever-necessary *simul* reminds us that politicizing the Christian life can be as much a distortion as depoliticizing it, privatizing it in the fashion of the late nineteenth century. Political obedience and civil disobedience both come under the judgment of the *simul;* the claim to be engaged in a righteous crusade, a crusade for Christ and country, or whatever slogan one wishes, is always to be called into question.

What the Germans in many ways failed to learn from the experiences of the 1930s, we in America have also tended to ignore. In recent years we have come very close to divinization of American political life. We are in grave danger of political idolatry. The agents of this idolatry, ironically enough, have often been conservative evangelicals. Until recently many of them have found the alliance with conservative politics very congenial. The formation of the People's Christian Coalition and the direction which its publication *The Post-American* is taking may indicate that this era may be ending. All Christians, whether conservative or liberal, must recognize that politics must remain limited; claims to absolute power must be called into question. We must keep political life in its proper place.

Thus it is not enough to assert God's sovereignty over the entire world. For this proposition taken by itself could easily lead to theocracy, to renewed emphasis on the notion of the Christian state. Precisely this understanding of their political life contributed greatly to the German catastrophe.

The point remains. Politics must be seen as a secular and limited enterprise.

More broadly stated, no human organization, no human arrangements—empirical religious organizations are also human arrangements—can ever be above criticism, can ever claim divine exemption. Institutions are made by humans and for humans; humans ought therefore not be made their victims.

The goals discussed in the previous chapter are paradoxically only possible where politics is seen as secular and limited, not as absolute. Thus we can claim that it is pluralistic institutions, the open recognition of diversity, that provides precisely for the freedom of the gospel that the conservative Christians so eloquently clamor for.

From a theological point of view this entire chapter can be seen as an extended commentary on the First Commandment. The prohibition against the worship of any created forms extends far beyond the sticks and stones, the graven images and the sacred groves associated with ancient paganism. Indeed to identify idolatry with the various symbolic representations of the divine, as some forms of left-wing Protestantism did during the Reformation, or with the use of ceremonies and vestments, is to miss the depths of the perversions against which the servants of Yahweh raised their voices millenia ago.

The basic options in the ancient world were limited, as indeed they are in our world. Idolatry then had two foci: fertility cults and political cults, mysteries surrounding the two great "givens" within which human life must be lived—our kinship with all living forms and the necessity for some orderly arrangement of our collective life. As George Mendenhall has so aptly put it, "the problem of demythologizing" (which is our task) "appears in a radically different light," once we realize "that the primary social function of the most important myths in antiquity was simply to indicate and promulgate the ultimate metaphysical legitimacy of existing social and power structures."

Mendenhall further spells out what the biblical witness implied in his discussion of the meaning of covenant. "The biblical covenant was a systematic proclamation that no one was in control, and every social organization was a secular business that depended entirely on its demonstrated value to human beings and its willingness to remain within the ethical bonds to which all members of the community were obligated." A Christian political stance, therefore, always has a double character: it is a stance on behalf of the neighbor in need and a stance that at the same time recognizes that the claim of the human goes beyond the claim of any political entity. In other words, the question of a Christian political ethic is always one of translating the ethical question into political programs without sacrificing the moral substance. It is, for example, the recognition that every Christian is called upon to work for peace, that in our day such work is inescapably political, and it is at the same time the recognition that no program for peace can in itself be identical with *shalom,* with the peace of God. For its authenticity, however, every program for peace must in some sense partake of the spirit of *shalom.* In the language we have used earlier, we live in constant awareness of the *simul,* of the broken yet gracefull character of all that we do; we struggle forward with such resources as we can bring to bear trusting at the same time that "in, with, and under" our efforts a steadfast love may carry us beyond our wildest dreams.

A Time for Disobedience

If a commitment beyond politics, beyond all created forms, defines the fundamental style of the Christian life, disobedience to existing social and political structures must be a continuing possibility. Theoretically Christian teachers and ecclesiastical potentates have always recognized the truth of this assertion. "It is better to obey God than man" remains one of the oldest traditions of the faithful. The difficulty, as in so many other instances, lies with its application, with its implementation. For directives of this kind are not automatically enforceable under conditions easily specifiable in advance. Indeed, any such claim would run contrary to the basic freedom of the gospel.

No one can order me to disobey an existing authority. That decision is a matter of individual conscience. It should be a conscience as well informed as possible. But a well informed conscience is not necessarily one crammed full with the latest socio-political data. The tests of relevance in moral issues are not just tests of fact; they are also tests of integrity, matters of fidelity to commitment. It should not require any great theological learning to know that one does not turn out of the house of God any person on the basis of race, ancestry, political persuasion, or any other external trait. Simple German burghers sometimes had better insight into this question than learned theologians who claimed to be true to the teachings of Martin Luther. It is faith after all that makes the witness, not learning. What is at stake is the integrity of the Word of God, not the correctness of a particular theological position.

The issue remains unchanged in our day. Thus civil disobedience will always be a voluntary matter. No religious organization can demand disobedience, though it may instruct the faithful so that they may understand their situation. Nor can any other organization demand disobedience, although those with similar understandings of a particular crisis may voluntarily band together and seek to instruct their fellow citizens. Indeed their consciences may compel them to make appeals of just this kind.

Civil disobedience takes on many forms. In each form it is both an act of faith and a political act. Thus, even though the act itself must be rooted in the decision of an individual conscience, no one can act without taking into account his relationships with his neighbors, with members of his household, his fellow believers, his fellow citizens, even his political enemies. Only if one has the illusion that one is acting in perfect righteousness can one ignore the larger context of one's action.

Nothing said here intends to suggest that there is no place for the lonely martyr. Such martyrdom is not, however, the predominant issue in our day. If anything, disobedience has been highly politicized. Thus it is its political ramifications to which we must particularly attend.

As a political form one of the primary expressions of civil disobedience in our day has been an act of *public witness.* Because much of what I shall say will appear critical of many of the participants in the organized protest movements of the 1960s, let it be said at the outset that without the public witness of civil disobedience neither the civil rights movement nor the wide-spread revulsion against the war in Vietnam would have been possible. *Public witness,* even acts which antagonists considered exhibitionist in nature, compelled large segments of the public to take notice. Montgomery, Birmingham, and Selma may count as paradigmatic events. Through them a largely indifferent white audience (for most whites were spectators, not participants) discovered something of the depth of racial injustice.

In citing these events as examples of civil disobedience I can rightly be called to task. For in every instance the protesting witnesses were legally vindicated. To know these outcomes is to know both the complexity of the issue in these matters and at the same time to recognize how little most white persons, including church leaders who should have been informed, understand not merely of racial injustice but of the structure of the American legal system and how one got justice to function. *For the public witness in which most black leaders engaged during the largest part of the civil rights movement constituted not disobedience but a summons to the American courts to enforce justice according to the Constitution.* Very few whites, especially in conservative circles, apparently understood this fact then nor understand it now. Thus the need for this kind of public witness persists.

The protests against the Vietnam war brought civil disobedience in a more clearcut form. Yet even here we must distinguish between the kind of acts which were intended to serve and actually did serve the purpose of extending the recognition of rights of conscience to persons previously excluded under narrow interpretations of the law and those acts which intended to challenge and change public opinion. Many of the protests clearly went beyond simply demanding that individual conscience be respected: these protests asserted that the war was itself a moral evil of vast dimensions. Their witness ran against collective involvement.

I have little doubt that most who protested against the war were sincerely against it. There is little value at this juncture in an agonizing scrutiny of consciences. Some measure of dissent from the war was probably given as thoughtlessly as much consent to the war was entered into. Under conditions of collective excitement, we should not be surprised at the existence of decisions of this kind.

But at the moment when protest moved from individual acts of conscience to calling the war itself into question civil disobedience entered the political arena on a scale which no individual act could equal. At this point not only considerations of principle but also questions of strategy and tactics became overwhelmingly important. Faith and politics had come together.

One cannot evaluate strategy and tactics except in the light of the mission they are to serve. The mission presumably was to end American involvement in the Vietnam war. Strategically such a mission required sensitizing the American public to the basic immorality of the war itself, mobilizing public opinion and political power against the war, and bringing about a decision in the Congress and/or the White House to terminate the war.

Initially these strategies required tactics of dramatic public witness in order to bring public attention around to the issues. Included in that witness, indeed necessarily a part of the struggle, if the judgment that the war was unjust was valid, was support of individual objectors to the war, not only through draft counseling—a perfectly legal and indeed constructive activity—but through the affirmation of the legitimacy of "conscientious desertion" (most of the Stockholm community) and political exile. Without question the development of resistance among those subject to the draft played a major role in sensitizing elements of the American middle classes. (The existence of class and race distinctions in the way in which selective service operated eventually worked against the resistance rather than in favor of it.) The public witness of the exiles became an important ingredient in the struggle against the war.

Unfortunately, though understandably, moral zeal sometimes made the protesters blind to the need for discussions of tactics. "Principle" apparently brooked no compromise. Thus some instances of public witness served to discredit the protesters rather than to arouse the consciousness of oppression. Similarly, both the Johnson and Nixon administrations, determined to maintain "order," overplayed their hands and resorted to the tactics of coercion.

The 1968 Democratic convention illustrates how principle escalated into confrontation. The troubles in Chicago may well have defeated Hubert Humphrey. Many of the protesters could have cared less at the time. After the first four years of Richard Nixon they may well have realized that tactically the hand was overplayed in Chicago.

Again it must be recognized that much of what happened in Chicago did not flow out of the tactical decisions of the opponents of the war. What happened at Chicago included a whole host of other issues and other grievances; it included also a good deal of flamboyant exhibitionism on the part of those who confused their personal bent with principle, their own compulsion to act with strategy, and their own eccentric behavior with tactics.

Both the McCarthy and the Kennedy campaigns in 1968 had underlined the fact that large numbers of Americans opposed the war in Southeast Asia. In 1968 those Americans did not succeed in reaching the goal they had set for themselves, capturing political power. But they had taken an important step. The pressures on Hubert Humphrey during the campaign, his movement, no matter how hesitant originally, towards the anti-war position, underscored the extent of the victory. The opportunity was not accepted.

It is of course easier to see how much had been gained after four years of Richard Nixon. To accuse Hubert Humphrey of surrendering to political expediency somehow seems less damning after George McGovern's difficulties in finding the appropriate form of expediency after his nomination, as well as in the light of the unprincipled appeal to expediency of some of the Nixon courtiers. Tactics are always a way of finding an expedient path to the goal. Some forms of expediency, however, sacrifice the goal for the sake of the momentary victory.

The tragedy, however, is that the counsels of expediency have brought the war in Southeast Asia to an end in such a way that almost all the issues of principle have been totally obscured. We have talked about "peace with honor" and failed to recognize the corrupting nature of American Imperialism. We have removed American fighting men without asking fundamental questions about American policy. Indeed the by-product of conservative reaction on the domestic front may be seen as partially providing the climate of assent within which the abuse of power on the part of the Nixon administration counted. These events helped bring the present constitutional crisis into being.

The worst of the Watergate problems, however, arise not out of events in Washington but out of the state of the public mind to which they testify. Watergate would be unthinkable in our national life without the unity of a kind of religious piety with exaggerated nationalism.

The best of conservative religion in the United States has always protested against this kind of identification, just as has the best of liberal thought. Unfortunately up to the present conservative evangelicals have had no ethical teacher of the stature of Reinhold Niebuhr to instruct them in political realism.

The new People's Christian Coalition may represent an emerging counterforce. Similarily we need to recognize the voices of existing evangelical spokesmen in public life, notably Senator Mark Hatfield of Oregon. At this juncture it may not be amiss to draw attention to his remarks at the 1973 National Prayer Breakfast. He challenged the gathering to "beware of the real danger of a misplaced allegiance, if not outright idolatry, to the extent that we fail to distinguish between the god of an American civil religion and the God who reveals himself in the holy Scriptures and in Jesus Christ." Senator Hatfield went on to remind his audience that "we sit here today as the wealthy and the powerful." He called upon them not to "forget that those who follow Christ will more often find themselves not with the comfortable majorities, but with miserable minorities." In these striking words from a national platform, the Oregon Senator put the basic issues clearly. Politics is a limited enterprise; there is no salvation in civil religion. The Word of God cannot be subsumed under any human authority.

Finally, whatever else may be said, we must recognize that loyalty to the Word of God always carries with it the possibility that we must say No to some existing social requirements or political demands. We dare not under any circumstances allow any element of the created order to become the focal point of human loyalties, human worship. This is the Protestant protest against idolatry, eloquently stated in Luther's explanation of the First Commandment in the Large Catechism, deeply rooted in the Old Testament understanding of the covenant with Jahweh.

I am in politics to help people. I must constantly be aware of the ambiguity of all efforts made in this direction. Politics is a worldly activity; it is not the Christian's ultimate concern; it may be his penultumate calling.

Notes on Sources

1. The material on Northern Methodists comes from Ralph E. Morrow, *Northern Methodists and Reconstruction* (East Lansing: Michigan State University, 1952). Quotations from *Luther's Works* are from the American edition. For the discussion of Luther's political ethics see Heinrich Bornkamm, *Luther's Doctrine of the Two Kingdoms in the Context of His Theology* (Philadelphia: Fortress, 1966), Heinst-Horst Schrey, ed. *Reich Gottes und Welt* (Darmstadt: Wissenschaftliche Buchgesellschaft, 1969) and Ulrich Duchrow, *Christenheit und Weltverantwortung* (Stuttgart: Klett, 1970.) I have also used Kjell Ove Nilsson, *Simul: Das Miteinander von Göttlichem und Menschlichem in Luthers Theologie* (Göttingen: Vandenhoeck & Ruprecht, 1966), tr. from the Swedish.

2. The historical materials are in Timothy L. Smith, *Revivalism and Social Reform* (Nashville: Abingdon, 1957) and Robert Bigler, *The Politics of German Protestantism* (Berkeley: University of California, 1972)

3. Reinhold Niebuhr, *Moral Man and Immoral Society* (New York: Scribner's, 1932) set the tone for Protestant realism.

4. Martin Luther King's letter can be found in *Why We Can't Wait* (New York: Harper & Row, 1964.) I have found very helpful Henry J. Pratt, *The Liberalization of American Protestantism: A Case Study in Complex Organizations* (Detroit: Wayne State University Press, 1972.)

5. James M. Gustafson, *The Church as a Moral Decision-Maker* (Philadelphia: Pilgrim Press, 1970.)

6. On "middle Americans" see Robert Coles, *Middle Americans* (Boston: Little, Brown and Company, 1971), Gabriel Fackre, *Liberation in Middle America* (Philadelphia: Pilgrim Press, 1971), Murray Friedman, ed. *Overcoming Middle-Class Rage* (Philadelphia: Westminster, 1971), and Peter Binzen, *Whitetown, USA* (New York: Vintage Books, 1970.)

7. See the two books which Francis Weisenburger has written about the last third of the nineteenth century: *Triumph of Faith* (Richmond, no publisher given, 1962) and *Ordeal of Faith* (New York: Philosophical Library, 1959.) I found very provocative Kenneth Clark's revolutionary slogan: "Just teach them to read!" *New York Times Magazine*, March 18, 1973, p. 14f. On the subject of diversity and equality I am deeply indebted to Theodosius Dobzhansky, *Genetic Diversity and Human Equality* (New York: Basic Books, 1973).

8. Dennis L. Meadows directed the Club of Rome study; see *The Limits of Growth* (New York: Universe Books, 1972). Every social ethicist recognizes the crucial importance of James M. Gustafson, *Christ and the Moral Life* (New York: Harper & Row, 1971.) Also very stimulating is James Sellers, *Public Ethics* (New York: Harper & Row, 1970.)

9. On the military-industrial complex see Max Stackhouse, *The Ethics of Necropolis* (Boston: Beacon Press, 1972.) On welfare problems see Jed F. Handler and Ellen Jane Hollingsworth, *The "deserving poor"; a study of welfare administration* (Chicago: Markham: 1971) and Frances F. Piven and Richard Cloward, *Regulating the Poor* (New York: Pantheon, 1971). Philosophically the discussions of objectivity in this chapter owe a great deal to Jurgen Habermas, *Knowledge and Human Interests* (Boston: Beacon Press, 1971) and Michael Polanyi, *Personal Knowledge* (Chicago: The University of Chicago Press, 1958.)

10. In addition to the references for chapter 1 I have relied on Eivind Berggrav, *Man and State* (Philadelphia: Muhlenberg, 1951), A. C. Cochrane, *The Church's Confession Under Hitler* (Philadelphia: Westminster, 1962), Ernst Wolf, *Barmen: Kirche Zwischen Versuchung und Gnade* (München: Kaiser Verlag, 1957), Hans Asmussen, *Zur Jüngsten Kirchengeschicte* (Stuttgart: Evangelisches Verlagswerk, 1961), Karl-Wilhelm Dahm *Pfarrer und Politik* (Opladen: Westdeutscher Verlag, 1965.) Bishop Dibelius' views can be found in *Obrigkeit* (2d ed.; Stuttgart: Kreuz-Verlag, 1963.)

See Henry Yoder, *The Politics of Jesus* (Grand Rapids: Eerdmans, 1972) and Sellers, *Public Ethics*. I have also profited from Peter Berger and Thomas Luckmann, *The Social Construction of Reality* (Garden City: Doubleday, 1966), Isador Chein, *The Science of Behavior and the Image of Man* (New York: Basic Books, 1972.) and George C. Mendenhall, *The Tenth Generation* (Baltimore: Johns Hopkins, 1973.) Niemöller's sermon is in *God Is My Fuehrer* (New York: Philosophical Library, no date) and Senator Hatfield's remarks can be found in *The Christian Century*, February 21, 1973.

DATE D